THE WITNESS BLANKET

Truth, Art and Reconciliation

CAREY NEWMAN
AND KIRSTIE HUDSON

IN MEMORY OF our friend Marilyn (Murray) Allison and to all of the Survivors and Intergenerational Survivors who shared their stories for the Witness Blanket. —C.N. and K.H.

Text copyright © Carey Newman and Kirstie Hudson 2022

Published in Canada and the United States in 2022 by Orca Book Publishers.
orcabook.com

All rights reserved. No part of this publication may be reproduced or transmitted in any form or by any means, electronic or mechanical, including photocopying, recording or by any information storage and retrieval system now known or to be invented, without permission in writing from the publisher.

Library and Archives Canada Cataloguing in Publication
Title: The Witness Blanket : truth, art and reconciliation / Carey Newman and Kirstie Hudson.
Names: Newman, Carey, 1975- author. | Hudson, Kirstie, 1976- author.
Description: Includes bibliographical references and index.
Identifiers: Canadiana (print) 20220175934 | Canadiana (ebook) 20220181241 | ISBN 9781459836129 (hardcover) | ISBN 9781459836136 (PDF) | ISBN 9781459836143 (EPUB)
Subjects: LCSH: Newman, Carey, 1975- Witness Blanket—Juvenile literature. | CSH: Indigenous peoples—Canada—Residential schools—Juvenile literature. | LCSH: Indigenous peoples—Mental health—Canada—Juvenile literature. | LCSH: Art therapy—Canada—Juvenile literature. | CSH: First Nations art—Canada—Juvenile literature. | LCSH: Installations (Art)—Canada—Juvenile literature. | LCSH: Reconciliation—Juvenile literature.
Classification: LCC E96.5 .N49 2022 | DDC j371.829/97071—dc23

Library of Congress Control Number: 2022933628

Summary: This nonfiction book for middle-grade readers, illustrated with photographs, tells the story of the making of the Witness Blanket, a work by Indigenous artist Carey Newman that includes items from every residential school in Canada and stories from the Survivors who donated them.

Orca Book Publishers is committed to reducing the consumption of nonrenewable resources in the production of our books. We make every effort to use materials that support a sustainable future.

Orca Book Publishers gratefully acknowledges the support for its publishing programs provided by the following agencies: the Government of Canada, the Canada Council for the Arts and the Province of British Columbia through the BC Arts Council and the Book Publishing Tax Credit.

The authors and publisher have made every effort to ensure that the information in this book was correct at the time of publication. The authors and publisher do not assume any liability for any loss, damage, or disruption caused by errors or omissions. Every effort has been made to trace copyright holders and to obtain their permission for the use of copyrighted material. The publisher apologizes for any errors or omissions and would be grateful if notified of any corrections that should be incorporated in future reprints or editions of this book.

Cover and interior design by Jacqui Thomas
Any photographs that are not credited are courtesy of Media One Inc.

Printed and bound in Canada.

25 24 23 22 • 1 2 3 4

CONTENTS

1   Pieces of History   1

2   Every Object Has a Story   13

3   I'm Hungry   21

4   Moccasins   27

5   Photographs   33

6   Kids Will Be Kids   41

7   Letters   49

8   More Than 100 Years   57

9   Fitting the Pieces Together   65

10   Reconciliation Is a Journey   73

Glossary   82
Resources   86
Acknowledgments   88
Index   89

1 PIECES OF HISTORY

MY TRADITIONAL NAME IS Hayalthkin'geme.

Through my father I am Kwagiulth of the Kwakwaka'wakw Nation from northern Vancouver Island, in British Columbia. Through his mother, I am Coast Salish from Cheam of the Stó:lo Nation along the Upper Fraser Valley. On my mother's side of the family, I am descended from English, Irish and Scottish **settlers** who planted their roots in Saskatchewan. I built the Witness Blanket, and this is the story of how it came to be.

opposite: JESSICA SIGURDSON, CANADIAN MUSEUM FOR HUMAN RIGHTS

Carey's father, Victor Newman, at the site of St. Mary's in Mission, BC, the last residential school he was sent to. MEDIA ONE INC.

My Family

Being of mixed heritage, I have always felt conflicted about my experience growing up in Canada. This country provided one side of my family with the opportunity for a better life. At the same time, **colonization** has damaged generations of my Indigenous relatives.

Before the first settlers came from Europe to North America, **Indigenous Peoples** had lived on and looked after this land since long before the Egyptian pyramids were built. During those pre-contact times there were hundreds of societies across the lands now called Canada. Among these ancient cultures there were distinctive beliefs, ceremonies, traditions and languages, most of which survive with today's First Nations, Metis and Inuit people—who are collectively known as Indigenous. I say "survive" because traditional culture and ways of life changed dramatically after colonization.

In 1867 Canada was formed when the British Parliament enacted the British North America Act.

> *In 1455,* the Pope made a declaration that lands not occupied by Christians were vacant and that Christians could claim those lands as their own. This is known as the Doctrine of Discovery and was used by European countries to colonize distant lands. In 1763, King George III claimed lands in North America for Britain.

That act contained the first laws dealing with Indigenous people, and an original copy of it is inside one of the wooden boxes that hang from the bottom of the Witness Blanket. The reason I put it there is that, besides taking away land and other rights, the act claimed responsibility for educating Indigenous children. In 1876 the Indian Act was signed with the clear purpose of assimilating Indigenous people and erasing their cultures.

These acts of colonialism affect me and my family in many ways. One way is through **residential schools**, which operated from the mid-1800s to the late 1990s.

My father was born in 1937 in the remote town of Alert Bay, British Columbia. At age seven he was taken from his parents and sent to a residential school far away from home. Residential schools were started by the Canadian government and run by churches. The goal was to erase Indigenous cultures by making children like my father think, speak and behave less like their own people and more like European settlers. At residential school my father wasn't allowed to speak Kwak'wala, the language of his people. He couldn't learn about their traditional ways of living or cultural ceremonies. School authorities wouldn't even let him talk with his siblings. Losing these experiences hurt his connection to family and culture. It also changed how he thought of himself and altered who he grew up to be.

Documenting the Truth

Many people who have suffered trauma don't like to talk about their experiences. This is true for my father.

top: Carey's grandmother, Mary Agnes Newman (nee Victor), with his aunt Georgina (left), aunt Doris (right), father Victor, in the striped shirt, and Victor's baby brother Ted. COURTESY OF THE NEWMAN FAMILY
bottom: Victor, Marion and Carey Newman outside their family home in Sooke, BC. COURTESY OF THE NEWMAN FAMILY

Carey with a collection of his artwork at age 13. COURTESY OF THE NEWMAN FAMILY

To protect my sisters and me from feeling his trauma, he has shared only a few details about his years at residential school, never telling us about the abuse he endured.

From the time he left for school to just before his 19th birthday, the adults in his life were mostly residential school supervisors. They were the only "parents" he knew, and his relationship with them influenced his relationship with my sisters and me.

Knowing that my father is a residential school **Survivor**, and that my sisters and I are **Intergenerational Survivors,** led me to want to know more about that part of Canadian history. So when the **Truth and Reconciliation Commission of Canada (TRC)** began in June 2008, I followed it closely. The TRC's purpose was to document Survivor experiences and tell Canadians what happened at residential schools.

Telling Our Story

I started learning to be an artist at age five, watching my father carve. I still remember the smell of cedar chips in his workshop. With his help I learned to make drawings and paintings that I would sell at the craft shows and markets he attended. At age 12 I made my first two editions of silkscreen prints, and from then until now, the only career I've ever known is being an artist.

When the TRC announced it was looking for commemoration projects, I wondered what I could make. How could I use my art to tell a story as big as residential schools in Canada? Most of what I do is carving from wood, stone or metal. I start with a big block or log and remove the parts I don't want, slowly revealing a mask, **totem pole** or sculpture.

I wanted to make something to represent the experience of Survivors. Canada is a big country, and more than 150,000 Indigenous children went to residential school. I needed to make something that wasn't just large as in tall or wide but was a concept big enough to carry thousands of stories. I had never created anything like that before.

Carey in his studio in 2018, carving details on a 36-foot (11-meter) red cedar totem. ANDREW QUERNER

Eventually I was running out of ideas, and, not knowing what to do, I sat down in my living room, resting my feet on a little folding stool. The part my feet were on is made from small pieces of wood strung together to create a flexible cradle. That gave me the idea of gathering objects from residential schools and Survivors across Canada. I thought, "I'll make something like this! But much bigger!"

I imagined a blanket made of these solid objects, strung together like my little folding stool. I knew that by gathering and then assembling these pieces like a huge patchwork quilt, I could make something that could tell the whole story.

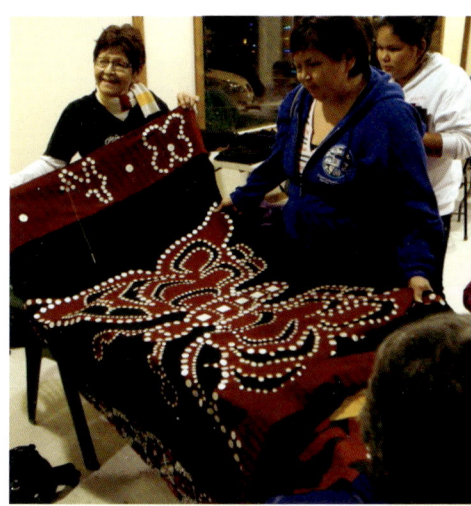

The Witness Blanket collection team visiting Alert Bay, BC, in January 2014. MEDIA ONE INC.

Wrapped in a Blanket

Blankets have great significance in both my Kwakwa̱ka̱'wakw and Coast Salish cultures. In my Kwakwa̱ka̱'wakw culture, our blankets show everyone who we are. We stitch symbols onto them that represent

Pieces of History ♦ 5

According to the TRC, from the mid-1800s to the late 1990s, more than 150,000 Indigenous children were forcibly taken from their families and sent to live at residential schools set up by the federal government and run by different religious groups.

A ceremony following the demolition of St. Michael's residential school in Alert Bay, BC, in February 2015. MEDIA ONE INC.

our family crests. We wear them in ceremony. They are part of our identity and display our lineage. In my Coast Salish tradition, we use blankets to honor, uplift and protect people. If somebody has accomplished something especially good for themselves or the community, we acknowledge their achievement by putting a blanket around them as a sign of gratitude. If someone has gone through trauma or falls on hard times, we do the same thing as a gesture of protection.

When I consider what blankets mean to the rest of the world, I think about how we wrap our babies in blankets when they're born, and how we often wrap our loved ones in blankets when they die. The blanket carries symbolic importance in almost every culture.

Bearing Witness

The name Witness Blanket came from something my wife, Elaine, heard on **CBC** Radio. A reporter was

interviewing people about a TRC event, and when he asked a priest why he was there, the priest said simply, "I'm here to bear witness." After hearing this, Elaine phoned me and said, "Bear witness, bear witness—it's about bearing witness." I looked up what it means to bear witness and found a definition that said "to show by your existence that something is true." It was perfect, because the project was about bearing witness. My role as an artist is to bear witness. The pieces themselves are witnesses. The people giving us the pieces are witnesses, and at some level we are all— or all should be—witnesses.

In both Kwakwa̱ka̱'wakw and Salish oral traditions, witnesses have an important role. Witnesses help us preserve history or important moments. In Kwakwa̱ka̱'wakw ways, we hold **Potlatches** to tell our stories, and then we give gifts to our guests and ask them to remember and share what they saw. In the Salish tradition, we ask people to stand as witnesses and speak about what they have seen and heard. We then give them tokens as payment to carry and remember our history.

Following that tradition, I created Witness Blanket coins to acknowledge people who made contributions or helped us along the way. Everywhere we went, we gave out the coins, which said "thank you" in many different languages.

Coming Up With a Plan

The Witness Blanket started with a very simple idea: one brick from every residential school across Canada.

Witness Blanket coins were given to those who made contributions to the Blanket.

Thousands of kids died at residential schools across Canada—so many kids, in fact, that having a graveyard next door to a residential school wasn't that unusual. Today thousands more unmarked graves have been found at residential school sites, surpassing the original number of recorded deaths.

Pieces of History ♦ 7

Carey fit the pieces of the Witness Blanket together like a puzzle. JOHN LEHMANN/ *THE GLOBE AND MAIL*

But how would I collect pieces from all these schools? How would I travel to so many communities and meet so many people from across the country? And how could I do all of that while at the same time building the Witness Blanket?

I realized I needed a team of people to help me. I hired three people to travel the country collecting items. While the collection team was on the road, I would stay close to home in Victoria, British Columbia, to work on the design, and another team would help me build the Blanket.

The finished Witness Blanket is about 39 feet (12 meters) long. The tallest point is over 10.5 feet (3 meters) high. And when assembled, the 13 panels weigh more than 2 tons (1.8 metric tons).

A Blanket Made of Solid Objects

The scope of the project was big. The collection team reached out to dozens of communities across Canada to spread the word about what we were trying to do. We wrote letters, advertised in different publications and held information sessions at the TRC hearings across the country.

At the beginning, when the Witness Blanket was just a concept and we couldn't show what it would look like, it was hard to describe exactly what we were making. People would ask, "How do you make a blanket out of solid objects? A blanket is supposed to be soft." Explaining the idea was a slow process, but I believed in the project and I was sure it was going to work.

Eventually momentum started to build, and word about the project spread. Often people needed time to think about what they wanted to contribute and would send an object in the mail weeks or even

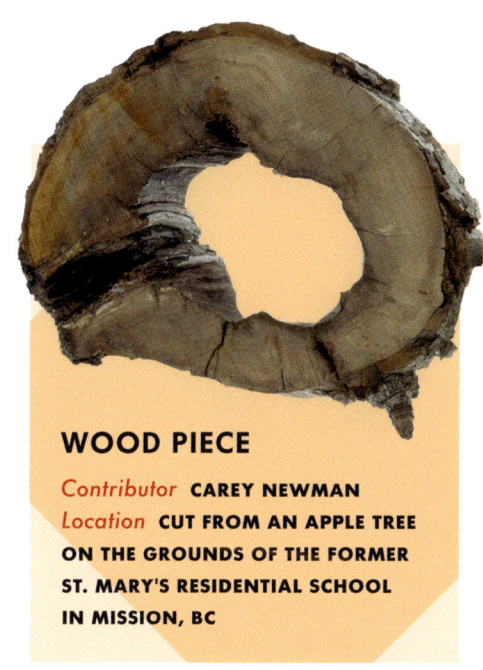

WOOD PIECE

Contributor **CAREY NEWMAN**
Location **CUT FROM AN APPLE TREE ON THE GROUNDS OF THE FORMER ST. MARY'S RESIDENTIAL SCHOOL IN MISSION, BC**

WOVEN IN

One day early in the project, an envelope arrived in the mail. In it were pieces of blue stained glass. They were the first objects we collected for the Witness Blanket. They came from the church at St. Eugene Mission, near Cranbrook, British Columbia. Those pieces of blue glass were photographed, recorded and safely stored away. We had started our collection.

Once a week I picked up the packages that had arrived at the Victoria Native Friendship Centre. Every week there were a few more than the week before. It was exciting to see objects coming in from all over the country and to read the personal stories attached to them. Seeing the diversity of pieces and stories, I knew the Witness Blanket was going to become something very special.

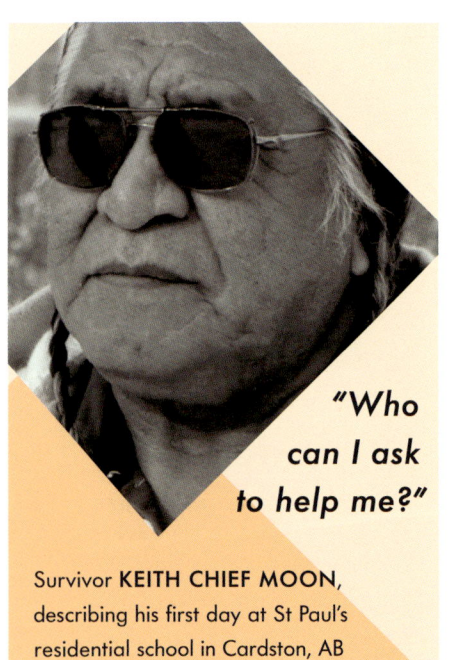

"Who can I ask to help me?"

Survivor **KEITH CHIEF MOON**, describing his first day at St Paul's residential school in Cardston, AB

months later. Other times the collection team would get an object right away. One of the first trips was to Nunavut, and the team came home with a prayer book, written in Inuktitut, from St. Jude's Cathedral in Iqaluit.

When we talked with Survivors and asked them to donate something to the project, they would put all sorts of things into our hands, objects that connected them with their own residential school experience, their own memories, their own stories. They would ask us if we would take these hockey skates, or these photographs, this pair of moccasins, a graduation certificate, a doll. We said yes. We took it all.

So Many Stories to Tell

Through meeting and talking with people, and keeping an open mind, I realized that the buildings themselves and what they were made from were just one part of the residential school history and experience. What is a brick without the story behind it?

Each of the pieces has a story of its own. One by one they tell individual stories of Survivors and Intergenerational Survivors and the ways in which residential schools harmed people and families in the past and continue to affect them in the present. Together they show the whole history of residential schools in Canada, including the government policy that made them, the churches that ran them and the damaging idea that Indigenous people should be taught to look and act and speak like the settlers who named this country Canada.

In the coming chapters, you will see and read about the pieces and stories that make up the Witness Blanket. You will meet some of the people we met along the way. Through their words and stories, you will have a chance to understand a little bit about what it means to be Indigenous in Canada today. Some of the stories might be sad, some will lift your spirits, and I hope that each one will teach you about an important part of our shared history.

Reverend Cyrus Blanchet, Jamie Lewis and Rosy Hartman collected a prayer book at St. Jude's Cathedral, Iqaluit, NU.
COURTESY OF THE WITNESS BLANKET TEAM

> "It has been strongly impressed upon myself, as head of the Department, that Indian children should be withdrawn as much as possible from the parental influence, and the only way to do that would be to put them in central training industrial schools where they will acquire the habits and modes of thought of white men."

Sir John A. Macdonald, first prime minister of Canada, who established the residential school system in Canada, speaking in 1879

Pieces of History ♦ 11

2 EVERY OBJECT HAS A STORY

WHEN I STARTED THE process of collecting pieces to make the Witness Blanket, I knew enough about residential school history to be prepared for how emotional the stories that came with them would be. I also knew I would need to be gentle with myself and the team, and that together we would need to be kind and caring with Survivors and other people who participated. Sometimes just asking people to talk about what they have experienced can trigger emotions and retraumatize them.

What I didn't anticipate or prepare myself for was the power held within the items themselves. I learned an important lesson early on when Rosy Hartman, one of the members of my team, brought me a piece she had collected. It was a child's shoe from the site of a burned-down residential school in Yukon.

opposite: The shoe as it appears on the Blanket. JESSE HLADY

Rosy Hartman with Harold Gatensby on the site of the Carcross (Chooutla) residential school in Yukon. MEDIA ONE INC.

There have been mission schools in Carcross, YT, since the early 1900s. The government-run residential school opened in 1911 and closed in 1969.

Harold's Story

The Carcross (Chooutla) residential school sat in a valley on the shore of Nares Lake, a short distance from the village of Carcross, Yukon. Harold Gatensby went to school there as a boy. Now he lives on the site where the school once stood.

Harold doesn't have good memories of his experience at the school. "I knew three things at 12 years old: I was stupid, I was ugly and I was going to hell," Harold said. "Those three things I knew for sure. Everything else was mixed up and confusing. That's what residential school did to me. I don't ever want any 12-year-old kid to be feeling like that."

Harold wondered what people would say now if kids were taken from their homes and families and put in a place where they didn't know anyone, where they didn't speak the language and where they got in trouble—not for something they did or didn't do but because of who they were.

"Maybe then they'll understand what it is that we carry in our hearts," Harold said.

He took Rosy for a walk on the land where the school once stood and shared his story with her. They collected objects for the Witness Blanket as they went. He pointed out an abandoned building that was the staff house for the school. He showed Rosy where the farm and the garden used to be. In a clearing, a concrete set of stairs from the boys' dormitory is all that's left of the original building.

Moss and Tree Needles

Harold led Rosy to a trail at the edge of the clearing. They had to push through branches and step over bushes to make a path through the forest. Every few steps they came across objects from the old residential school. There were washtubs, rusty old gas cans, cooking pots, glass bricks from the windows and even a bed frame. The forest was slowly growing up around them and hiding them from view.

Harold stopped, noticing something small. He turned and faced Rosy. "Maybe you'd like this," he said. He pointed to a leather child's shoe, almost covered over by the forest. It was warped from years of being out in the weather. It was covered with moss and tree needles. Rosy gently took it in her hands.

The day after she returned to Victoria, there was a knock at my door very early in the morning. It was Rosy.

"Something's got to be done about this horrible legacy we've inherited."

Survivor **HAROLD GATENSBY**

Every Object Has a Story ♦ 15

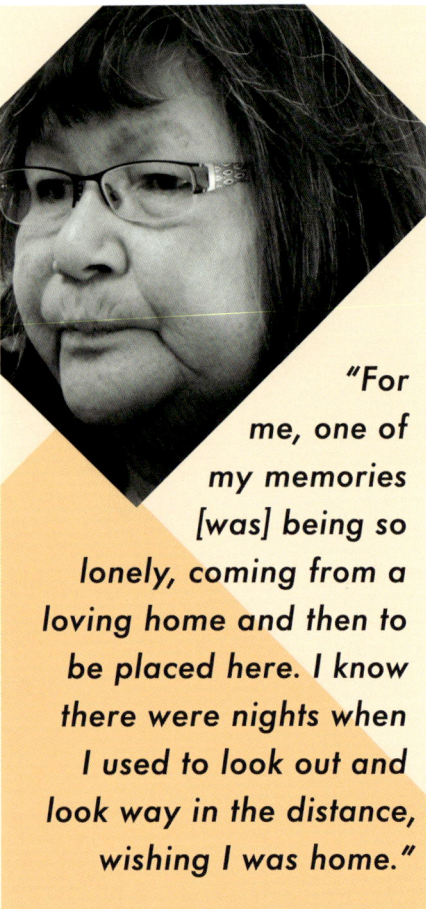

"For me, one of my memories [was] being so lonely, coming from a loving home and then to be placed here. I know there were nights when I used to look out and look way in the distance, wishing I was home."

Survivor ANGELINE AYOUNGMAN

She was holding a little box, and inside it was the small, disfigured and moss-covered leather shoe. She explained that the evening she'd collected the shoe, she had woken up in the middle of the night feeling afraid. She'd been running from something in her sleep. The nightmare really scared her. The night she returned home, her husband had the exact same scary dream. She thought, "It has to be the shoe."

Now that I had it, I wasn't sure what to do. What if my family or I had the nightmare? Were the scary dreams really caused by this little shoe? If they were, was I doing the right thing by bringing all of these pieces together? That evening I went down to my workshop, took out the box and removed the shoe. I remember the powerful wave of sadness that filled me as I held it. Objects don't often make me feel that kind of emotion. But I still get tears in my eyes when I think about that shoe, maybe because it makes me imagine my own father when he was small enough to wear it.

Holding the shoe, I tried to imagine what it would be feeling if it were a person, scooped up from the forest, put in a box and carried a long way from home. Almost like a child taken to residential school. What I sensed wasn't exactly anger—it was mostly fear.

BRAIDED SWEETGRASS

Contributor **FILE HILLS QU'APPELLE TRIBAL COUNCIL HEALTH SERVICES**

Location **FORT QU'APPELLE, SK**

JESSICA SIGURDSON, CANADIAN MUSEUM FOR HUMAN RIGHTS

WOVEN IN

Having the shoe arrive early in the process taught me an important lesson. I had to respect the power of objects, stories and people equally. That experience changed my way of thinking. It changed the way I handled the items we collected. It changed my creative process and the final work itself. From that point on, rather than seeing those items as just a bunch of random "things" that I was sticking on this Blanket, I recognized each object as sacred.

It became part of my routine to take a moment to connect with each piece as it came in. I went through all of them, one by one. I held each object, feeling its weight and shape in my hands. I learned their stories and thought about how they were similar or different. I thought about how to transform them to fit them together and fasten them to the Blanket. I measured them and recorded the information I would need to include for each one.

I knew I had to treat them with care. I knew it was important to place them on the Witness Blanket with some sense of equality. I couldn't simply take the ones I liked because of their color or their shape, or because of how much I liked their stories or the people who contributed them. To properly reflect their unique and **collective truth**, I needed to treat them all with dignity and respect.

Rosy Hartman, from the Witness Blanket team, collecting a child's shoe from the forest floor in Carcross, YT. MEDIA ONE INC.

> **Most of** the residential schools were built of the same red brick. Even the buildings themselves looked the same, with standardized floor plans. If you walked into a residential school on Vancouver Island, the classrooms, kitchen, bathrooms and sewing room would be in the same place as they were in a school in Shubenacadie, NS.

What Stories Would They Tell?

Not knowing what else to do, I began to speak about the project. There I was, trying to deal with my own fears and doubts while also trying to calm the unsettled feeling that came with this little shoe. I talked about what I was doing, about my ideas, about my vision for the Witness Blanket. In a way I was asking for the shoe's approval, but saying those things out loud also helped me clarify the project in my own mind.

I repeated that process each night for the next week or so. Each time, the emotion I sensed from the shoe was different. I started out a little afraid, both because of the story Rosy had told me and from taking on this enormous project. I had never done anything this big or important to so many people before, so I wasn't confident I would know what to do. Slowly my fears were replaced with a sense of responsibility. As I talked about the project and what I had to do, the Witness Blanket became clearer in my mind.

Like all of us, each of these objects were witnesses. In addition to the stories that their contributors shared, the pieces had untold stories of their own. They were there, part of residential schools, silent observers of the events that took place. A brick, a shoe, a doorknob, a bowl, piano keys, a hockey skate, a moccasin or merit badges. What had each of these objects seen? If they could speak, what stories would they tell?

top: Carey figuring out where and how to place items on the Blanket. MEDIA ONE INC. *bottom:* Hundreds of cedar blocks were cut and sanded to form the shape of the Witness Blanket. MEDIA ONE INC.

The Witness Blanket team went to every province and territory, traveled over 124,000 miles (200,000 kilometers), visited 77 communities and met over 10,000 people. Along the way they gathered more than 889 pieces of history, including documents, braids of hair, merit badges and piano keys.

Every Object Has a Story ♦ 19

3 I'M HUNGRY

THERE'S A YELLOW BOWL on the Witness Blanket. It's small and simple, but it tells a much bigger story. It's a story about what food represented at residential schools across Canada—not just the quality of the meals that were served but, in many cases, whether there was even enough food to go around. This is a topic that comes up again and again when Survivors talk about their experiences.

The bowl is made of plastic. It comes from a residential school called the Mohawk Institute, in Brantford, Ontario. Students who went there call it a mush-hole bowl. Mush is a type of thick porridge that was regularly served to the students. And because of how often it was served, "mush hole" became the nickname of the school.

opposite: JESSICA SIGURDSON,
CANADIAN MUSEUM FOR HUMAN RIGHTS

Girls and boys sit at separate dining tables at Little Buffalo residential school at Lubicon Lake, AB. SHINGWAUK RESIDENTIAL SCHOOLS CENTRE, ALGOMA UNIVERSITY

A food historian named Dr. Ian Mosby uncovered documents about nutritional testing that went on at residential schools in Canada starting in the 1940s. They show that government officials experimented on at least 1,300 Indigenous kids. In some of the studies, one group of kids would be given vitamins, while another group wouldn't get them.

Sour Milk

Food is a big part of our daily lives. Many of us associate the smell of a particular food with memories of people, places or experiences we've had. The students who went to residential schools across Canada are no different. I have my own memories about food that are connected to my dad's experience at residential school.

To this day there are certain things he can't or won't eat. He hates scalloped potatoes because at residential school they were made with sour milk and weren't fully cooked. Today, even if they are perfectly cooked, with the freshest ingredients, because of his negative memories my dad still won't eat them.

At residential school students were often forced to finish everything on their plates. That's how it was at my house too when I was growing up. I was told that if I didn't eat my dinner, I would be served the same food for breakfast.

When I was four or five, I ran away from home because I refused to eat liver. At that age, running away meant packing my Hot Wheels cars in my backpack and riding my bike to the end of the driveway, because I wasn't allowed out of the yard. Although I laugh now when I tell that story and describe my older sister, Marion, running after me and yelling "Don't go, don't go," I also see how that experience shaped my relationship with food for years to come.

A Box of Apples

Richard Lucas said it didn't matter what school you went to, the food—or lack of food—was the same. He went to Christie residential school in Kakawis, British Columbia, when he was seven. And, like my dad, even as an adult he still won't eat certain foods.

He said if the boys got an orange, they would often eat the peel. Even though it tasted awful, at least they were able to get something in their stomachs. In many cases it became necessary for the kids to learn how to steal food, not because they were bad children but because it was the only way for them to survive. Often they weren't only taking food for themselves; they were looking out for each other, making sure everyone had something to eat, at least enough to fend off hunger for a little while.

"We knew the way to the kitchen porch where the carrots [and] turnips were," Richard said. "If you worked in the kitchen, you'd go hide a box of apples and oranges so you could get it at night."

Richard can't smell a hot breakfast without thinking of his time at Christie. "You could smell the bacon and eggs cooking, you could smell the toast and the coffee,"

> "They often talked about the simple little things. A piece of food, a plate, a dish—stealing an apple in order to feed themselves or somebody else, a crust of bread."
>
> Senator **MURRAY SINCLAIR** on what he heard from Survivors as chair of the Truth and Reconciliation Commission hearings

Dr. Peter Bryce was hired in the early 1900s by the **Department of Indian Affairs** in Ottawa to report on health conditions at residential schools in Western Canada. His report, which was critical of the schools, was never released. He was fired from his job, but he published his findings in another report, *The Story of a National Crime: Being a Record of the Health Conditions of the Indians of Canada from 1904 to 1921.*

I'm Hungry ♦ 23

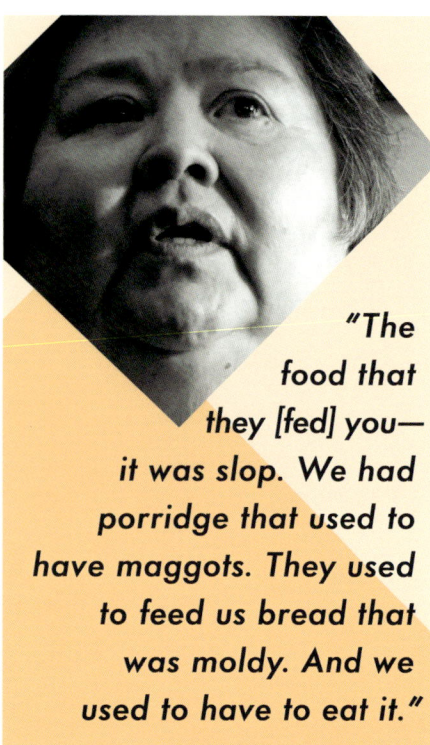

"The food that they [fed] you—it was slop. We had porridge that used to have maggots. They used to feed us bread that was moldy. And we used to have to eat it."

Survivor **NANCY WAMISS**

The dining rooms at most residential schools were divided—the boys sat on one side and the girls sat on the other. Even though the boys and girls weren't allowed to talk to each other, they would often secretly pass food across the hall. And sometimes the dessert or a piece of bread would get eaten before it made it to the right person.

he said about the food the staff ate. "We never had that at Christie, not once."

While the students were doing what they could to get enough to eat, many Survivors, like Richard, say the people working at the schools had a very different diet. All the beautiful food that was being grown on the **industrial school** farms, including fresh vegetables and fresh meat, would pass by the students' dining halls on its way to the nuns, priests and staff. Meanwhile, the students were served moldy bread, cold food and watered-down soup.

Food Lessons

Even now, my dad's experience with food at residential school affects me and my family. For example, because I was taught not to waste any food, it's still hard for me not to eat everything I am served. At a restaurant, if there are six french fries left, even when I am completely full, I feel the need to finish them.

When I had a child of my own, I realized that I was teaching her those same harmful eating habits. My wife, Elaine, helped me understand that I wasn't allowing our daughter to listen to what her body needs. Everyone should be taught to trust that they know when they are full. I also learned that giving her all the unhealthy food she wanted wasn't good for her and could lead to poor eating habits as an adult. It hasn't been an easy lesson for me to learn, but thankfully—for both her health and mine—we are figuring it out as a family.

MEDIA ONE INC.

WOVEN IN

In addition to the simple, plain mush-hole bowl, ornate dishes were donated to the Witness Blanket, including a silver sugar bowl and creamer from the Mohawk Institute. There are two cake plates from the Sechelt residential school in British Columbia. One has a strawberry design, the other a plum design. These dishes weren't used by the students. I wanted to show the difference between the plain dishes used by the children at the schools and the fancy dishes used by staff, priests, nuns and supervisors. When I was designing the Blanket and deciding where and how to use each piece, I chose to keep the humble yellow bowl whole, the way it was when it was given to me. I am not sure if it was a conscious decision, but I cut the cake plates into pieces. When I look at it now, I can see that by keeping the bowl whole and cutting the fancy plates apart, I was expressing my disapproval of the unfairness they symbolized. I was also honoring the true experience of the students.

4 MOCCASINS

THERE'S A PAIR OF tiny moccasins made by girls at the Edmonton industrial school in St. Albert, Alberta, mounted in one small box on the Witness Blanket. Anne Nelson donated them to the project. Her mother was a student at the school for six years. Anne's mother was given the moccasins, which she then gave to her daughter.

Anne's grandfather was the first principal of the Edmonton industrial school, which sat on an 855-acre (346-hectare) farm. It was open from 1924 to 1966, and the kids who went there had school in the morning and farming and housework in the afternoon. The work the kids did running the farm produced most of the food they ate there.

opposite: JESSICA SIGURDSON,
CANADIAN MUSEUM FOR HUMAN RIGHTS

Florence Mary Dodman and some of her siblings. COURTESY OF MARILYN (MURRAY) ALLISON

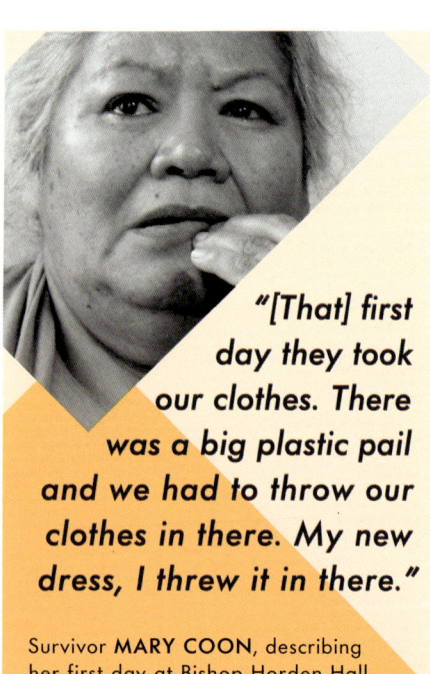

"[That] first day they took our clothes. There was a big plastic pail and we had to throw our clothes in there. My new dress, I threw it in there."

Survivor **MARY COON**, describing her first day at Bishop Horden Hall residential school in Moose Factory, ON. Mary never saw her dress again.

Alice's Moccasins

Florence Mary Dodman was born in 1927. She went to Fort Resolution residential school, also known as St. Joseph's, in the Northwest Territories in the late 1930s. Florence started at the school when she was about nine years old, and she stayed there until she was 15. Her three-year-old sister, Alice, and baby brother, Jimmy, started at the same time.

Florence's daughter, Marilyn (Murray) Allison, said her mother did not share a lot about her time at the school, just a few stories over the years, including one about her first day. "Her first experience when she entered the residential school was [of] all these children crying and crying and crying," Marilyn said. "[They were] all lined up in beds, just like you see in the pictures."

28 ♦ The Witness Blanket

WOVEN IN

Along the way we gathered quite a collection of different textiles, and I had to think about how to include them on the Witness Blanket. I wanted people to touch and feel the objects, but I didn't want the delicate things like moccasins and tea towels to be harmed by the dust of travel and the oil of curious hands. My solution was to design shadow boxes with plexiglass windows to protect the most fragile items.

There was one textile item I couldn't bring myself to change or take apart to fit the Blanket—a girl's sweater from a residential school uniform. I didn't want to cut it. That sweater had warmed a young girl at a residential school somewhere in Canada. If I had cut off an arm or even part of a sleeve to fit it on the Blanket, it wouldn't have meant the same thing. It needed to stay whole. The only way to understand the power of that sweater was to see it whole. I made a special box for it so that it

MEDIA ONE INC.

could travel as part of the Witness Blanket exhibit. I did the same thing with a few other objects that were too big and too special to cut down to a size that would fit on the Blanket.

One of the memories of residential school that Florence liked to share with Marilyn was of picking berries in the summer. Marilyn remembered her mom talking about how she and the other girls loved the berry picking because they were all together and outside and they got to nibble a few themselves. And even though the berries they picked were for the nuns, not the children, Florence would talk about that experience fondly.

One cold day in Fort Resolution, Florence and her sister, by this time six years old, along with all the other kids at the school, were locked outside to play. This was a common occurrence at St. Joseph's, but

> **Some residential** schools were called industrial schools. They were designed to train students for jobs as unpaid laborers. The girls would spend half their school day cooking and sewing, while the boys would spend the same amount of time working the fields or tending the livestock. Much of what they produced was then sold to help pay for the operation of the school.

Merit badges were handed out at residential schools starting in 1942. They looked like the badges you earn at Brownies or Scouts, but they weren't the same. They recognized skills that students mastered for things such as cooking, cleaning and gardening—skills that had no connection to their culture.

By 1944, 1,493 merit badges had been issued at residential schools across Canada. Eight of those badges ended up on the Witness Blanket. Survivors said they are proof of slavery at the schools.

above: JESSE HLADY

on this day, Alice was very sick, and it was extremely cold outside. She was feverish and couldn't stop coughing. Florence pounded on the doors for help. Finally one of the nuns opened the door and let Alice inside. That was the last time Florence ever saw her little sister.

Passed Down through the Generations

That day haunted Florence for the rest of her life. No one ever knew exactly what had happened to Alice. A long time after the day she was locked out of the school, the family was finally told that Alice had died. Even then, they didn't know what Alice had died of or where she was buried.

A year before Florence died, she pulled out an old shoebox of keepsakes to show Marilyn. Inside was a pair of tiny moccasins, small enough for a baby. They were embroidered with purple, pink and white flowers. Each moccasin had a pair of white braided tassels. Florence said they were made by her own mother, or possibly her grandmother, for the first-born child in her family.

"They were passed down to each child," Marilyn remembered her mom saying. "Every child wore those moccasins, down to the youngest child." That meant Florence would have worn them, and Alice too, and every family member who went to residential school. Marilyn held on to those moccasins until she contributed them to the Witness Blanket in honor of her mother.

I like to think about that little pair of moccasins as a reminder of life and culture before residential school. They reach across time and speak to the love and comfort of family.

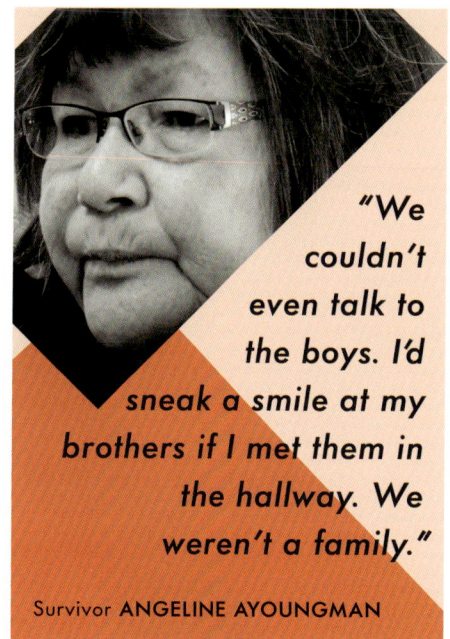

"We couldn't even talk to the boys. I'd sneak a smile at my brothers if I met them in the hallway. We weren't a family."

Survivor ANGELINE AYOUNGMAN

MOCCASINS

Contributor **MARILYN (MURRAY) ALLISON**

Location **ST. JOSEPH'S RESIDENTIAL SCHOOL, FORT RESOLUTION, NT**

5 PHOTOGRAPHS

THERE ARE MORE THAN 150 photographs on the Witness Blanket. Some of them are class photos, similar to the ones taken at any school today. Most of them are in black-and-white and show students and scenes at residential schools across Canada. Although I can see by the images themselves that they represent many decades of history, I don't know exactly when a lot of them were taken. I can only guess by the quality of the image and take clues from the clothes the kids are wearing.

One of the oldest ones comes from Coqualeetza residential school in Chilliwack, British Columbia. The 10 boys in the photo are dressed in three-piece suits with ties or bow ties. Their hair is parted in the middle, a style that was popular in the 1920s. The two girls are in long skirts and double-breasted jackets.

opposite: JESSICA SIGURDSON, CANADIAN MUSEUM FOR HUMAN RIGHTS
above: COURTESY OF COQUALEETZA CULTURAL EDUCATION CENTRE

left: A class photo from St. Peter's Anglican Mission, Lesser Slave Lake, AB, circa 1920. PROVINCIAL ARCHIVES OF ALBERTA (A14802)
right: A close-up of the boy on the far left ended up on the Blanket. MEDIA ONE INC.

> **There are** 161 photos on the Witness Blanket and hundreds more that travel with the exhibit. Each one represents some part of the residential school experience. I chose them based on the story they could tell.

Another photo shows a group of younger kids bundled up against the cold at Whitefish Lake residential school in Alberta in 1937. The girls are wearing toques, but the boys aren't. They have their scarves crisscrossed across their bodies. In a photo from Lesser Slave Lake residential school in Alberta, 26 kids of all ages are standing in front of a school with three of their teachers. The girls are wearing collared dresses, and they all have a similar bob haircut. The boys are in shorts, leggings and boots. Some of them are wearing blazer jackets. Their heads are shaved.

All the kids are looking at the camera except one—a boy of about eight or nine who is off to one side. His head is down, shoulders hunched, and he is looking at the ground. When I was fitting the images onto the wood blocks for the Blanket, that's the part of the picture I focused on.

One Little Village

In the 1920s a boat called the *Bonita* (which is Spanish for "beautiful") traveled back and forth across Lac La Ronge in northern Saskatchewan. It ferried up to 40 Indigenous kids from one side of the lake to the other. Every September for decades, kids as young as five climbed into the boat and left their communities behind for another school year. They were all going to the same place, Lac La Ronge (All Saints) residential school, on the south side of the lake.

The only way to get to the residential schools on Lac La Ronge, SK, was by boat. GENERAL SYNOD ARCHIVES, ANGLICAN CHURCH OF CANADA

Tom Roberts said back then it would take some families half a day just to make the journey to where the *Bonita* or a boat like it picked them up. The route they took had four portages along the way. At every **portage**, the families would climb out of their boats, carry them over land to the next beach and continue the next leg of their journey.

"At the end of that last portage, they'd put their kids into this big boat, never to see them again for 10 months," Tom said. "How sad that journey must have been for the parents, when they went back home with no kids in their boat. It's like the Pied Piper who took all the kids away from that one little village."

No One to Tuck You In at Night

The *Bonita*, and many other boats like it, would ferry the kids back to their families the following spring, when the school year was done. The boats carried kids

BRASS DOOR KNOB

Contributor **THE GOVERNMENT OF NOVA SCOTIA**
Location **HALIFAX, NS**

WOVEN IN

It took a long time to work out how to include the pictures, and the memories they represented, on the Witness Blanket. I wanted to find a way to include them without damaging any of the originals. There's a photo of a boy dressed in full **regalia**, kids on a playground, young girls working in a garden, a group of boys brushing their teeth in a washroom. There are archival shots of schools, snapshots of mealtimes in dining halls and pictures of hockey teams.

I also felt it was important for me to include photos of my own family. There are pictures of my aunts and uncles and grandparents. There's a black-and-white photo of my dad. He's sitting under a Christmas tree, between his brothers and sisters. He told me he was about five or six in that photo, and it was from the last Christmas he spent at home before he went away to residential school. When I look at it, I imagine what it would have been like for him to leave his family and have his life so completely changed in first or second grade. I think I can understand why he doesn't want to talk about that last Christmas at home.

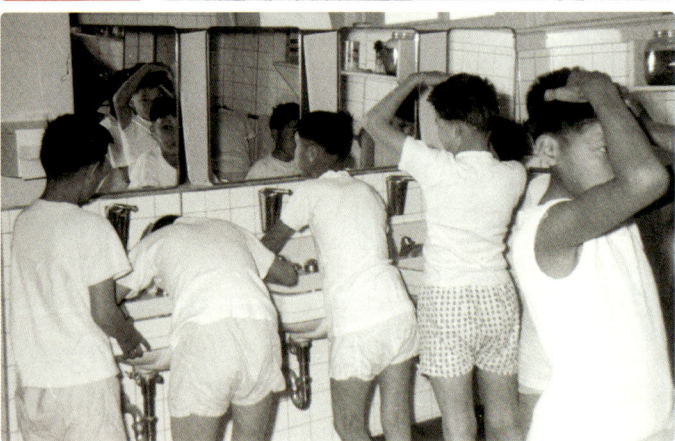

top: COURTESY OF THE NEWMAN FAMILY
middle: SASKATCHEWAN ARCHIVES BOARD (R-A8223)
bottom: NWT ARCHIVES/SACRED HEART PARISH (FORT SIMPSON) FONDS (N-1992-255:0082)

The finished image blocks were mounted on the Blanket. MEDIA ONE INC.

to and from the residential school on Lac La Ronge starting in 1907, and continued until the school burned down in 1947 and the students at All Saints moved to a new school in Prince Albert, 124 miles (200 kilometers) away.

Tom said his first day at All Saints was the saddest day of his life. He went there when he was seven or eight years old. Tom said he got very, very lonely. "You don't know until you get there that your mom and dad aren't there to tuck you in at night," he said.

One of Tom's lasting memories from All Saints was being told that because he was Indigenous, he couldn't do certain things. He said the staff at the school would say to him, "You're nothing but an Indian, you'll never be able to do it." Tom said he and his friends would play games of cowboys and Indians, but no one ever wanted to be the Indian.

When Tom talks to young Indigenous students now, he always brings the black-and-white photo of the kids packed into the boat. The photo tells a

"My mom and dad weren't there. I couldn't talk to my brother, I couldn't talk to my sisters. I wasn't the only one crying. There were lots of kids crying, wanting to go home, not tomorrow or next week, but right now."

Survivor TOM ROBERTS

Photographs ♦ 37

Students in a classroom at St. Mary's residential school on the Blood Reserve in Alberta. COURTESY OF LANCE SCOUT

story about one residential school in northern Saskatchewan, but it's just one of the many hundreds of photos that were donated to the Witness Blanket. And like Tom's photo, each of them came with their own story to tell.

Families Broken Apart

As the team traveled the country, gathering objects for the Blanket and talking to Survivors, we found many people who were willing to share their stories about residential school. They often shared experiences and memories that, like my father, they couldn't or wouldn't share with their own families, their own kids. Maybe it's better that I don't know exactly what happened to my dad. Maybe it's easier for my soul to

> **According to** the Truth and Reconciliation Commission, there were 139 residential schools in Canada. They operated from the mid-1800s to the late 1990s. That number doesn't include **day schools** or schools that were run provincially.

38 ♦ The Witness Blanket

The Federal Tent Hostel in Coppermine, in what is now Kugluktuk, NU. The hostel opened in 1955 and had space for 30 Inuit kids, who were billeted in eight tents. Permanent schools weren't often built in the Arctic because foundations couldn't be dug in permafrost, so this photo is one of the few remaining records of that school.

GENERAL SYNOD ARCHIVES, ANGLICAN CHURCH OF CANADA

hear about the kinds of things that happened to him through the words of other Survivors.

Tom Roberts said he went to residential school as a child and came back as an adult, just like his grandfather, mother, uncles and aunties before him. Many people still don't know there was a residential school on Lac La Ronge. In fact, there wasn't just one—over the years there were many in that area. Even though it's part of Tom's story, he still can't imagine kids being taken away from their families at such a young age. "Mom and Dad there, sitting at home, couldn't do nothing," Tom said.

In 1920 the federal Indian Act made it mandatory for every Indigenous child in Canada to go to residential school. It was illegal to go to any other type of school.

6

KIDS WILL BE KIDS

LIFE AT RESIDENTIAL SCHOOLS across the country followed a similar pattern. The days were typically made up of school, chores and church. If there was time left over at the end of the day, that's when the kids could sometimes just be kids, even if it was only for a little while.

Many Survivors shared stories of how sports—hockey, baseball, skiing, running—helped them get through their time at residential school. Many of the objects we collected for the Witness Blanket tell that part of the story. Children at the schools could sometimes have fun playing sports, creating art, making music, inventing imaginative games or doing something else that allowed them to escape their harsh reality.

opposite: JESSE HLADY

above: A boys' hockey team from the Lejac residential school in Fraser Lake, BC.
COURTESY OF RITA MICHELL
below: Athletes at residential schools excelled in all kinds of sports. JESSE HLADY

Lacing Up Their Skates

One piece that stands out for me is the Gordon's Golden Hawks Ladies Hockey Tournament championship trophy. It came from Gordon's residential school in Punnichy, Saskatchewan. The trophy is from 1996, the last year that school was open, making it one of the newest objects on the Blanket.

There are four other photographs relating to hockey. Two of them are formal team photos with the players lined up in their uniforms. One team is from the Lejac residential school in Fraser Lake, British Columbia, and the other is from southern Alberta. Somewhere in a box of childhood keepsakes, I have a similar photo of me playing hockey as a boy.

top: Boys at the Edmonton industrial school get ready to play hockey. PROVINCIAL ARCHIVES OF ALBERTA (A13454) *inset:* Marek found this skate in the hallway of the residential school in Lestock, SK.

There is also a photo that shows a group of boys standing on the ice in their skates, holding their hockey sticks. Although they are all wearing newsboy caps instead of helmets, they look like they're getting ready for a game. The photo doesn't have a date on it, but you can see the Edmonton industrial school in the background.

There are even two old-fashioned hockey skates on the Witness Blanket. I mounted them in front of pictures of hockey teams. From the style of the skates, it looks like they're from the 1970s. They came from

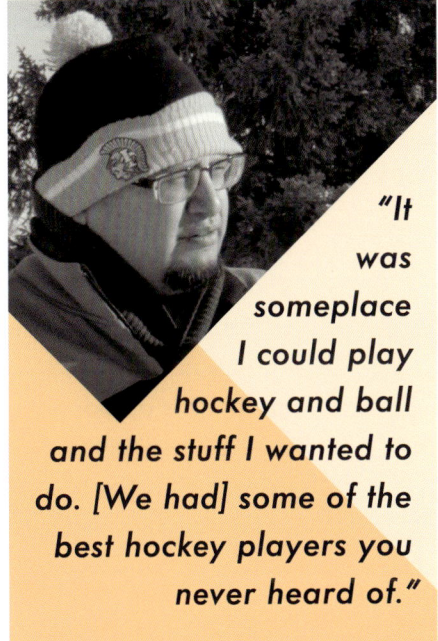

"It was someplace I could play hockey and ball and the stuff I wanted to do. [We had] some of the best hockey players you never heard of."

Survivor **LEON WOLFE**

Kids Will Be Kids ♦ 43

COURTESY OF RITA MICHELL

WOVEN IN

I mentioned that there are four photographs on a panel with the hockey skates. The reason I described only three of them is that I was saving my favorite for last. It is a color photo, peeking out from behind the lower of the two skates. In it is a group of boys in a field of slush and melting snow. They are all wearing gumboots and holding sticks and brooms, and they're covered in mud after what I imagine was a spirited game of broomball.

When I was making the Witness Blanket, I was often overwhelmed by the sad and tragic stories I heard. In those moments when I felt my mood darken, I would look at that picture, and those beaming smiles were sunshine for my soul. Collectively, these stories are little pieces of humanity amid a lot of despair. I love how they illustrate the incredible resilience of human nature and remind me that kids will always find a way to be kids, even in the most difficult of circumstances.

Art Thompson was an internationally known artist and master carver. On the Witness Blanket is a large painting he did as a boy at the Alberni residential school in British Columbia. It might be his earliest surviving work of art. His instructor there was a man named Robert Aller. The reason some of Art's paintings are still around is that Mr. Aller, who kept meticulous records, saved them. JESSE HLADY

the abandoned Muscowequan residential school in Lestock, Saskatchewan.

Making Their Own Fun

There weren't a lot of things for the younger kids to play with at residential school, so they had to make their own. When Bob Charlie attended the Whitehorse Baptist Mission residential school in Whitehorse, Yukon, from 1950 to 1956, the other kids who were there came from all over the territory.

In the winter they made their own skis and toboggans. "You'd get planks of wood, sand them down, put them on the barrel stoves and bend them," Bob said. Because the hill they zoomed down ended

DOLLS
Contributor **PHYLLIS OLNEY ACKLES**
Location **ALERT BAY, BC**

Kids Will Be Kids ♦ 45

Girls at a residential school on the Blood Reserve get together for some carol singing.
GLENBOW ARCHIVES (NA-5190-8)

Gordon's residential school in Saskatchewan was one of the last residential schools in Canada to close its doors, in 1996. The building was demolished not long after.

up on the road, they had to watch for cars. One boy would always be the lookout, stationed at the bottom of the hill. If a car was coming, he would warn the boys at the top of the hill.

Hockey for Hours

Bob's mother died when he was six months old. He lived with relatives for a few years, but when he was four he went to the orphanage at the residential school. When he turned six, he started school. The six years Bob spent at the school weren't easy. He had some bad experiences there, and sometimes, even all these years later, he remembers things he'd rather forget.

But there were moments when Bob could just be a kid, flying down the hill on homemade skis. Those are the memories he focuses on. He did his school work during the day and then did chores, like chopping wood and carrying it to feed the double-barreled stoves in the dormitories. After that he would lace up his skates. "You would play hockey for hours," Bob said. They had organized teams that were so good they were unbeatable for years in a row. The teams in Whitehorse used to get frustrated because they couldn't beat the boys from the residential school.

Art Thompson was one of the first people to describe his residential school experience in the Supreme Court of Canada. What he and a few other Survivors shared with the judges opened the door for more Survivors to come forward and share their stories. Those efforts pushed churches and the Canadian government to finally acknowledge their role in what happened at those schools.

Teacher Robert Aller surrounded by art students at a residential school.
COURTESY OF UNIVERSITY OF VICTORIA LEGACY ART GALLERIES

"You had to create your own entertainment... [We] would play hockey for hours."

Survivor **BOB CHARLIE**

Kids Will Be Kids ♦ 47

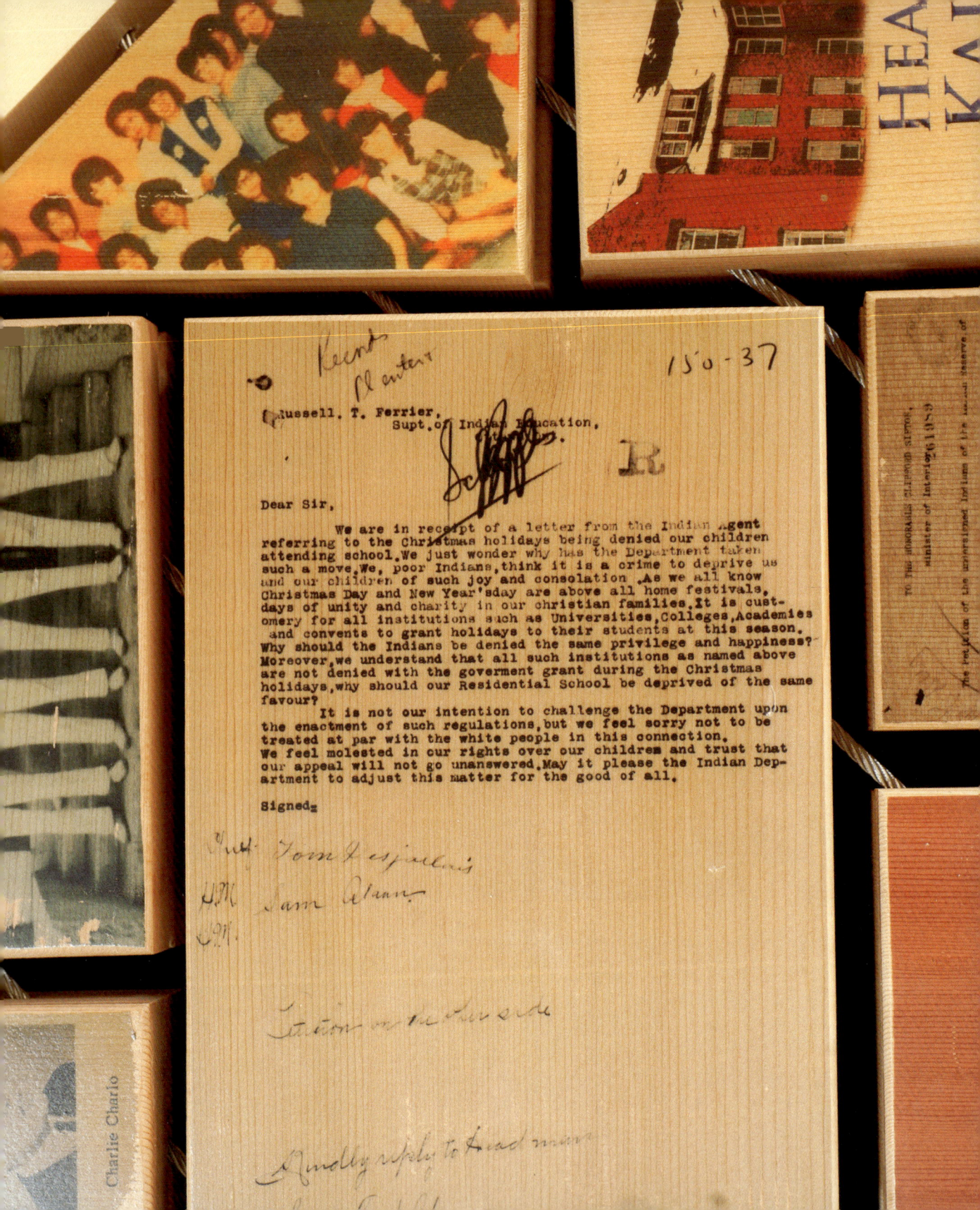

7 LETTERS

I WANTED THE WITNESS BLANKET to include one thing from every residential school in Canada. At the end of our travels, though, after collecting pieces for the project from coast to coast to coast, we were still missing items from several schools.

There were any number of reasons why we couldn't track down any objects from or memories of those schools. In some cases, the actual school buildings didn't exist anymore—or were never permanent structures in the first place. In other cases, despite our efforts we were unable to connect with Survivors who attended them.

opposite: JESSE HLADY

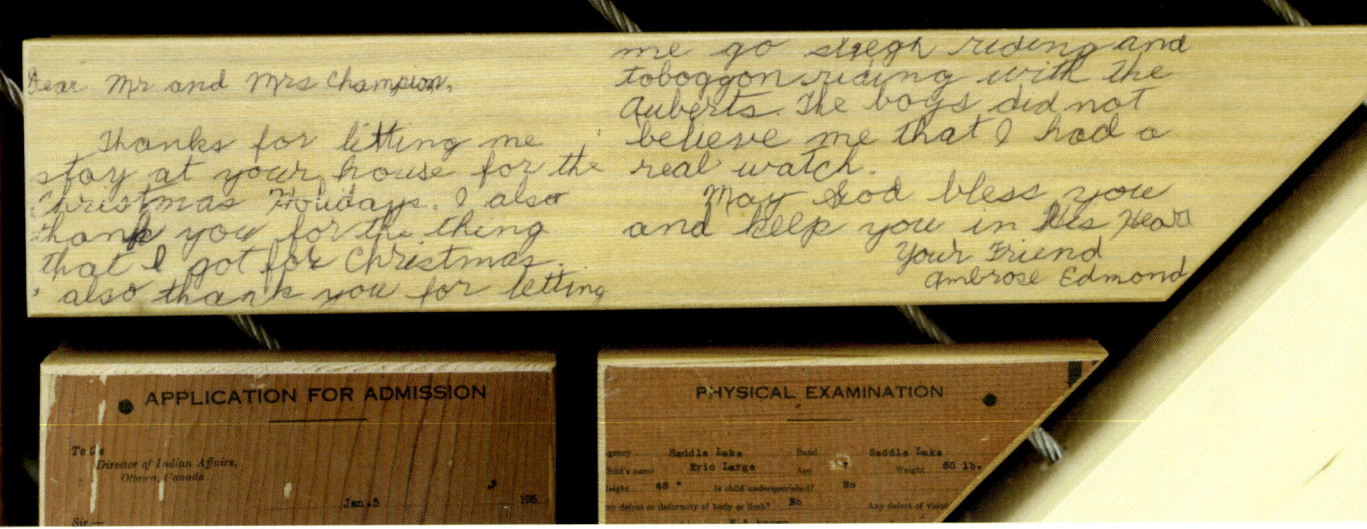

Ambrose Edmonds wrote this thank-you letter from his residential school in Mission, BC, in 1965. JESSE HLADY

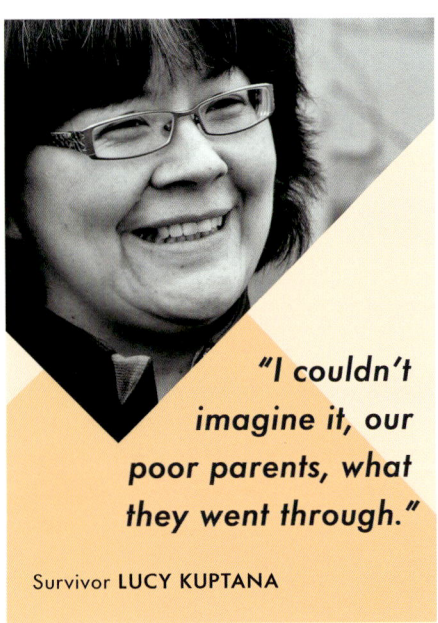

"I couldn't imagine it, our poor parents, what they went through."

Survivor **LUCY KUPTANA**

Looking for Evidence

We had been given documents such as school records, graduation certificates and yearbooks. Documents like these gave me the idea of finding other documents in government and church archives. We came across building inspection reports, memorandums listing school supplies for the coming year, letters from students and pamphlets outlining school rules. In the case of one school, we found only one mention of it in all our digging. It was an invoice for coal to heat the school in the winter.

When the Blanket was almost done, we were still missing pieces from six schools. We knew they had existed, but we couldn't find any physical objects, photos or documents mentioning them. It was important to have representation from every single residential school in Canada, because when the buildings that housed those residential schools are torn down or crumble into history, the Witness Blanket will remain as part of the permanent record. Thankfully, the research team at the **National Centre for Truth and Reconciliation** was able to find something we could use from each of the six missing schools, but even though we eventually met our goal, I decided to leave some empty spaces for the stories yet to be told and objects that came in after the Blanket was complete.

Chief Woomastoogish's Letter

Of the many documents on the Witness Blanket, one series of correspondence tells a particularly tragic tale. On June 29, 1919, 12 young boys from Bishop Horden Hall residential school in Moose Factory, Ontario, climbed into one canoe. They were trying to cross the Moose River to Hazey (now Hayes) Island, a distance of about 547 yards (500 meters), to go berry picking, a distance of about 547 yards (500 meters). The canoe flipped over in the river, and seven of the boys drowned. Their names were Alfred Loutitt, Thomas Loutitt, Arthur Sutherland, James Sutherland, Harry Wesley, John Sailors and Sinclair Nepaneshkum.

Chief Woomastoogish of the Moose Band wanted to know why and how so many small boys from his community had died. He wrote a letter in his own language, using **Cree syllabics**, to a man named Duncan Campbell Scott at the Department of Indian Affairs. Chief Woomastoogish wanted to make sure Scott understood two important things about this tragic accident: the 12 children in the canoe had no adult

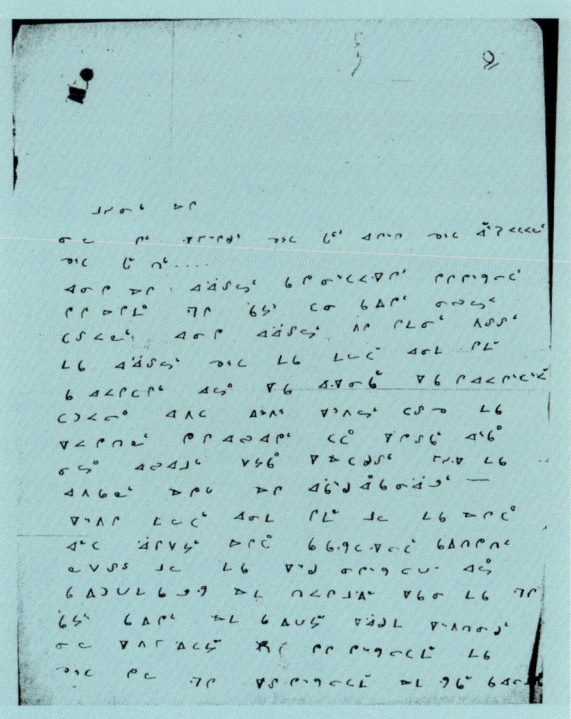

Chief Woomastoogish's letter to Duncan Campbell Scott. SHINGWAUK RESIDENTIAL SCHOOLS CENTRE, ALGOMA UNIVERSITY

> *"It is hoped that this accident will not result detrimentally to the future recruiting of pupils for the school."*
>
> Government official **A.J. MACKENZIE** in a letter to the principal of Bishop Horden Hall school about the drownings

Letters ♦ 51

> **More than 6,000 students died in residential schools across Canada, but many people suspect the actual number is much higher. In 2021 the remains of 215 children were found on the grounds of the former Kamloops residential school.**

supervision, and the canoe they were using wasn't fit for anyone to use, much less a large group of young boys.

"These children were allowed to go crossing the river every day in it and very often twice in one evening," wrote Chief Woomastoogish in his letter. "The canoe which they were using was very bad. The canvas of the canoe was half ripped." The canoe should not have been out on the water in that condition, so it's not surprising that it flipped when it was overloaded with 12 boys.

No Clear Answers

This series of letters was contributed by the Shingwauk Residential Schools Centre at Algoma University in Sault Ste. Marie, Ontario. As I read through them, I was struck by the difference between how Chief Woomastoogish saw the tragedy and how the officials in Ottawa handled it. The letters detail the story of seven young lives lost. They also highlight the actions of a 14-year-old boy named John Carpenter from the Fort Hope Indian Band who saved the life of an eight-year-old boy by holding him above the water until help arrived. They tell us that Carpenter was awarded a medal for his bravery. However, what is missing is any recognition of the original letter from Chief Woomastoogish and the concerns he raised about why those boys were in that canoe on that day in the first place. Instead, government official A.J. MacKenzie wrote to the principal of the school that the deaths of the boys were regrettable. He agreed that one canoe should never have held that

BRASS LAMP

Contributor CHIEF WILLIAM CRANMER AND COMMUNITY MEMBERS
Location ST. MICHAEL'S RESIDENTIAL SCHOOL, ALERT BAY, BC

WOVEN IN

I often think about Chief Woomastoogish's letter to Duncan Campbell Scott at the Department of Indian Affairs. What was he thinking as he wrote it? How did his community cope with the deaths of not one but seven young boys? "There was not one boy big enough to have any sense," Chief Woomastoogish wrote in his letter. "I don't know if this report was sent in yet or not, but this which I say is exactly what happened, and this is the weight which I am carrying."

John Carpenter was every bit the hero described, and valor like his deserves recognition. But I think the government officials in Ottawa, instead of stopping at a letter of commendation and a medal for bravery, should have held the staff at Bishop Horden Hall accountable. As a father myself, I would want to see a safety plan implemented. At the very least they could have provided a safe canoe.

many kids but concluded that the school staff weren't to blame for the accident.

Love Notes

Stan and Nancy Wamiss met at St. Michael's residential school in Alert Bay, British Columbia. Stan said he lost much of his childhood in his time at the school, including being deprived of family and culture. When he went home from school in the summer, his dad would be carving canoes. But because of how he'd been taught to think at residential school, Stan chose to play with his friends rather than learn from his dad.

"We never paid attention to our culture," Stan said. "When I left residential school, my dad died and took everything with him, his knowledge. What I'm learning now in our culture, I should have known when I was 10 or 12 years old, you know?"

> "We wish to have our children brought back from the above-mentioned school and to attend the day schools in our **reserve**. We would rather see … our children attend them than to have them so far away and being poorly treated."
>
> **CHIEF COUNCILLOR CORNELIUS BIGNELL** from The Pas Indian Band in a 1944 letter on behalf of the parents in his community, complaining about conditions at Elkhorn residential school in Manitoba

> "The servings fall very short in respect to eggs, cheese, liver, citrus fruit or tomatoes, the use of whole wheat or Canada Approved bread, butter and iodized salt."

Findings from a 1947 report about the food served at Chapleau residential school in Ontario, compared to the Canada Food Rules from that time

There are 102 documents on the Witness Blanket and hundreds more in a slideshow that travels with the exhibit.

All these years later, Stan and Nancy are married, and Stan is reclaiming his culture. He has even made his own canoes, just like his dad did. Whenever Stan thinks about residential school now, he tries to focus on the good memories, especially the ones that include Nancy and the times when they could just act like kids together.

"I used to send her love notes," Stan said. "We put things on a note, like I-T-A-L-Y: I Truly Always Love You. H-O-L-L-A-N-D was another one: Hope Our Love Lasts And Never Dies." The letters between Nancy and Stan tell a happier story. Sitting with them, listening to them talking, I noticed that when they shared difficult stories they were somber, their eyes

Nancy and Stan Wamiss met at residential school when they were kids.
MEDIA ONE INC.

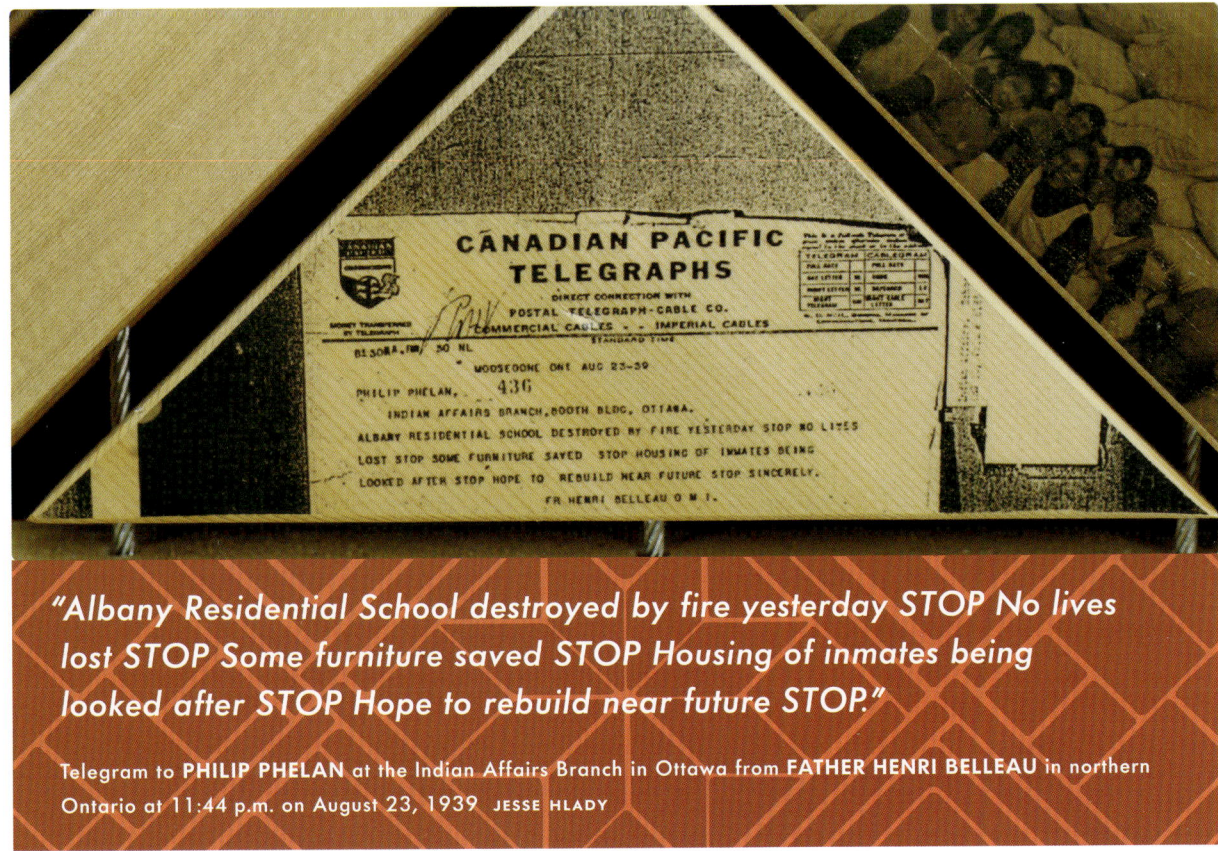

"Albany Residential School destroyed by fire yesterday STOP No lives lost STOP Some furniture saved STOP Housing of inmates being looked after STOP Hope to rebuild near future STOP."

Telegram to **PHILIP PHELAN** at the Indian Affairs Branch in Ottawa from **FATHER HENRI BELLEAU** in northern Ontario at 11:44 p.m. on August 23, 1939 JESSE HLADY

cast downward, but when they told us about those notes, they looked at each other, and I could see the love sparkle in their eyes. We all laughed together, and it was like medicine for our hearts.

8 MORE THAN 100 YEARS

ONE SHADOW BOX ON the Witness Blanket contains items connected with my family. There is a small feather that belonged to my grandmother, Aggie Victor. There are several old photographs of my dad and his family from when he was young. The one in the middle of the box is the photo of him and his three siblings from their last Christmas at home. There is also a leather book cover made by a man named Jerome Parnell. He was an amazing artist. He was also the biological father of my younger sister, Ellen, and an Intergenerational Survivor. Lastly, the box includes two braids of hair from my sisters, Marion and Ellen.

opposite: JESSICA SIGURDSON,
CANADIAN MUSEUM FOR HUMAN RIGHTS

Elder Shirley Alphonse cutting Marion's and Ellen's hair with their mother's help.
MEDIA ONE INC.

> "There is nothing simple about a haircut in my culture. It is a time for letting go of the past and starting fresh again. Mourning what is lost and moving forward. It is a mark of survival and growth through a painful time."
>
> MARION NEWMAN, Carey's sister

My Sisters' Braids

I wrote the following words for a film called *Picking Up the Pieces: The Making of the Witness Blanket*. It describes why my sisters gave their braids to the Blanket. "A common method of extinguishing cultural identity was to cut the children's hair when they first arrived at residential school. Survivors from across the country, including my father, shared stories of this difficult and traumatic experience. In many Indigenous cultures, hair is identified with strength and is only cut during times of mourning. My sisters, Marion and Ellen, decided to honor our father and other Survivors by cutting their hair and contributing the shorn braids to the Witness Blanket."

If you look closely at the braids, you can see a residue of red powder. It is a traditional medicine called ochre, and it is from the hair-cutting ceremony. Ellen's preparation began a year before the actual ceremony.

From the moment she decided to cut it, she was more aware of her hair than she had ever been before. "I became more thoughtful of what my hair actually means to me," she said. Marion describes the hair-cutting ceremony like this:

> My sister and I bathed in the clear river waters from melting glaciers for four sunrises in a row, while offering our prayers. On the fifth sunrise, sitting next to the fire that our father built, facing the ocean and the hills at our family home, we had our braids cut off as we cried our sorrows away.
>
> We cried for our father's loss of his childhood. We cried for our grandparents, our aunts, our uncles and our cousins who were all torn apart by their experiences at residential schools. We cried for our culture and the sense of self and well-being that was removed from all of those beings at such a young age...
>
> We cried until our tears ran to happy tears. Happy that we are able to walk free and live as we wish to, surrounded by a loving and healthy family and our beautiful culture that managed to survive a near obliteration.
>
> On the sixth and seventh days we rose to pray at sunrise over our hair, which lay outside on cedar boughs, sprinkled with ochre. On day eight our brother took our hair and wrapped it in red cloth. My sister and I brought the cedar boughs our hair had rested on to the river and let it wash away, taking our grief and worries with it.

The Sixties Scoop refers to a time from the 1960s to the mid-1980s when more than 10,000 Indigenous children were taken from their families and fostered or adopted by mostly non-Indigenous people. The Sixties Scoop is a legacy of the residential school system.

Losing Your Identity

The ceremony Marion describes was an emotional moment. I can still picture the smoke swirling around, embracing and connecting us. I remember

METAL SIGN

Contributor **ED D. BITTERNOSE**
Location **GORDON'S RESIDENTIAL SCHOOL, PUNNICHY, SK**

small details like the crackle and hiss of the fire. But clearest of all, I remember hearing the rasp of the scissors as Shirley Alphonse, the **Elder** and spiritual woman who performed the ceremony, began to cut the first braid.

"It felt like a part of me, my body, my spirit, was being cut and removed," Ellen said, describing that moment. "And I immediately thought of all those children, scared and torn from their families, who had their identities stripped from them."

Having their hair cut was a poignant experience for my sisters, and the sacrifice they made that morning will reverberate through their lives for a long time to come.

If you consider all the kids who went to residential schools across Canada in a period lasting for more than 100 years, it's easy to see why these kinds of experiences continue to ripple outward and be felt generations later by their children, their grandchildren and thousands upon thousands of Indigenous people who didn't ever go to residential school.

A Stranger at Home

One of the books donated to the Witness Blanket is called *Stranger at Home*, by Christy Jordan-Fenton and Margaret Pokiak-Fenton. It's based on a true story

top and middle: Carey's sisters, Marion and Ellen, cut their hair to honor their father and all the other children who had their hair cut off when they first arrived at residential school. MEDIA ONE INC. *bottom:* Marion throws the ceremonial cedar boughs into the river after the ceremony. MEDIA ONE INC.

WOVEN IN

My sisters' words speak to how closely we associate our hair with our identity and self-image. They cut their hair in ceremony, surrounded and supported by family. What would it feel like if your braids were suddenly cut off without your consent? Especially if it happened on your first day at a new school, surrounded by strangers? As I have said before, our father doesn't often talk about his time at residential school, but when he decided to go and give his statement to the Truth and Reconciliation Commission, the first story he told was about having his head shaved. Seventy years had passed since his first day at Sechelt residential school. All these decades later, his hands still trembled at the memory, and as he spoke those words out loud, he wiped tears from his eyes.

When my sister Ellen reflects on the experience, she says she learned "how important it is to tell people's truths, to hear them—really hear them." She says sometimes we need to "just sit silently with those truths. That until we sit in the spaces which are uncomfortable, until we honor those experiences, we cannot have true **reconciliation**. And that this is a lifelong journey." That is a piece of wisdom we can all learn from.

from Aklavik (Immaculate Conception) residential school in the Northwest Territories. It tells the story of a girl coming home from residential school and not fitting in anymore. She speaks a different language and dresses in strange clothes. Her mom doesn't recognize her and says, "Not my girl."

This was the experience of many kids who went away to residential school—all they thought about was when they could go home again. But what happens when, like the girl in the story, they get home only to learn they don't fit in anymore? And what happens when a parent can no longer recognize or connect with their own child?

> **Intergenerational trauma** happens when parents pass some of their fears or bad experiences down to their children.

Marion's and Ellen's braids are mounted in Carey's family box on the Witness Blanket.
JESSICA SIGURDSON, CANADIAN MUSEUM FOR HUMAN RIGHTS

The Indian Residential School Settlement Agreement (IRSSA) is a legal agreement between residential school Survivors, churches and the Government of Canada. It came into effect in 2007 and led to the creation of a multi-billion-dollar fund to help residential school Survivors with their recovery.

Stories like this say so much about how residential schools hurt Indigenous families. What does that loss of family and community turn into? In these cases, and many others, it turned into generations of parents who didn't know how to love their children because they themselves didn't feel loved.

I Love You

When the Witness Blanket was on tour, I took it to the Canadian Museum for Human Rights (CMHR) in Winnipeg, Manitoba. While it was being installed, an Elder there shared a story with me. She said when she learned that she was going to have a baby of her own, she was afraid she wouldn't know how to love

Empty dormitory in one of the Blood Reserve residential schools in Alberta.
GLENBOW ARCHIVES (NA-1811-54)

her child because she couldn't remember getting love from her own mother. She and her mother were both residential school Survivors.

When this woman was pregnant, she would look in the mirror and practice saying "I love you" over and over again. Imagine having to practice something like that. The love between a parent and a child is something we like to think comes naturally. The woman said all of her practicing in front of the mirror worked. Now she has grandchildren, and when they see her they say, "I love you." Those words seem so simple, but they are hard to say if no one has ever said them to you before.

> "In spite of the odds against it, we have survived. It is surprising that we have survived the hardships that we have encountered. We have survived to this point in our lives. We can declare our survival. And we will tell the story of our journey to this survival."
>
> Translation of a message written in the Blackfoot language by **ELDER CHARLIE CROW CHIEF** on a monument to Survivors from the Blood Tribe in Alberta

9 FITTING THE PIECES TOGETHER

THERE'S A WHITE WOODEN door right in the middle of the Witness Blanket. Because of its size, brightness and placement, it's the first thing you see when you stand in front of the Blanket. The door came from the boys' **infirmary** at St. Michael's residential school in Alert Bay, British Columbia.

Like the many other objects we collected, the door was in my studio for a long time before I finally figured out how I wanted to use it. I wanted to physically connect people with the experience of residential school, with the things we imagine when we look at the objects. If people couldn't touch all the objects (some are behind glass), then that big wooden door could become the way to create that experience.

opposite: CAREY NEWMAN

MEDIA ONE INC.

St. Michael's residential school in Alert Bay, BC, was demolished in 2015. The decision to take it down had created controversy. Some people wanted to knock it down, while others wanted to transform the space into something new. I think that no matter what a community decides, transforming how the space is used is the way to reclaim it from the past.

I wanted people to be able to put their hands on the doorknob, push open the door and walk through. I wanted them to think about the little kids who turned that same doorknob, pushed open that same door and walked through to the other side. If I put the door right in the middle of the piece, I could get people to do that and see for themselves what was on the other side.

Dark Hallways and Peeling Paint

It was dark inside St. Michael's residential school in Alert Bay. I had to use a flashlight to find my way around. The power had been turned off because the building had been condemned. There were sections of the building we couldn't even go into because it was too dangerous. After years of neglect and water damage, some sections of the floor could have collapsed underneath us. The walls inside were bubbling with moisture and age. Paint was peeling. Piles of wood

Carey inside St. Michael's, taking the infirmary door off its hinges. MEDIA ONE INC.

and pieces of furniture were stacked in the classrooms. Chairs were overturned in the hallways, and wires from the electrical system were hanging from the ceilings.

On a rainy, gray January day, with the wind blowing through the broken windows, rustling and swirling around and through us, there was an eerie feeling in and about the school. It was almost as if there were spirits from the past guiding us through the old building.

There was a big group of us touring the school that day. It included residential school Survivors, people from the community and our team from the Witness Blanket project. We were there to hear stories from the Survivors and collect objects before St. Michael's was torn down. We collected many things, including the big wooden door from the boys' infirmary, the object that would become the centerpiece of the Blanket.

The Mohawk Institute in Brantford, ON, was one of the oldest and longest-running residential schools in Canada. It accepted its first boarding students in 1831 and closed its doors in 1970.

Fitting the Pieces Together ♦ 67

> "Papa took my hand and I looked back and saw our chimney spurting smoke. I realized I wouldn't be there for the final fire before they left for a winter in the bush. It struck me that I wouldn't go with them at all, and I squeezed his hand tighter as we walked to school."

Excerpt from *Up Ghost River*, by Survivor **EDMUND METATAWABIN**, about leaving for his first day at St. Anne's residential school in Fort Albany, ON

The last residential school closed in the late 1990s. Since then some of those buildings have been knocked down. Some are empty and abandoned, while others have been reinvented as something completely new.

So Many Secrets

It was important to travel to Alert Bay that day and gather objects myself. I went to the places I had a personal connection with, and Alert Bay is my home territory. It's where my father was born. He didn't go to St. Michael's, but many of my family members did. My dad went to Sechelt residential school on the Sunshine Coast and St. Mary's residential school in Mission, British Columbia. After traveling to St. Michael's, I went to those places as well.

On that day at St. Michael's, Survivors shared stories about their experiences there. One man talked about how, when the building was used for band administration, some people wouldn't come to visit him in his office. Eventually he learned it was because his desk was set up in the former boys' infirmary. He moved his office the next day. He said that over the years many Survivors have talked about the abuse they suffered inside that room. It was a space that held a lot of bad memories for people.

I was walking through the building, picking up things from different rooms that either were visually interesting or had some connection to a story I had heard. When I walked along the dark hallway past the door to the infirmary, I stopped. I knew this was a significant part of the history of the building. Because the building was coming down, I had been given permission to take anything I wanted, so I decided to take the whole door.

Loading the infirmary door into Carey's truck. MEDIA ONE INC.

The Blanket Takes Shape

Taking a door off its hinges isn't easy. I walked out to my truck to get my tools. I went back to the door and carefully pulled the pins from the hinges and wrestled it out of the door frame. The door was heavy, and I had to carry it down three flights of stairs to get it to my truck. Dennis, one of the Survivors who had shared a little bit of his story that day, saw me struggling and offered to help. He picked up one end of the door and helped me carry it outside. It felt significant that he was the one who helped me remove it from St. Michael's.

Together we put the door in the back of my truck, and I brought it to my studio in Victoria, where it stood waiting for me to understand its purpose.

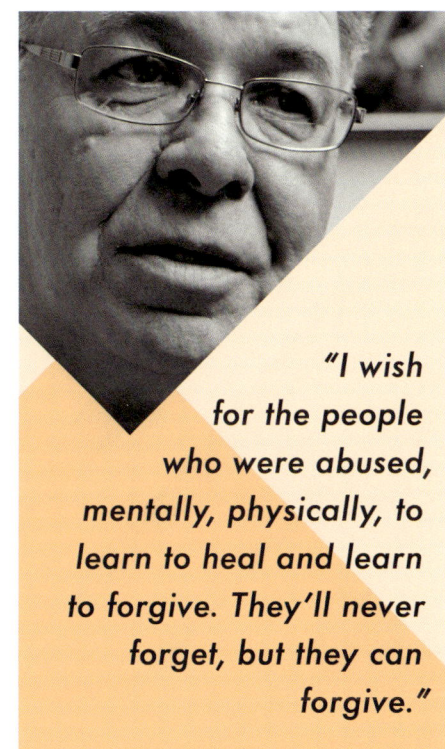

"I wish for the people who were abused, mentally, physically, to learn to heal and learn to forgive. They'll never forget, but they can forgive."

Survivor **TOM ROBERTS**

Fitting the Pieces Together ♦ 69

WOVEN IN

On my big art pieces, I always try to find somewhere for my daughter, Adelyn, to make her mark. After the Witness Blanket was finished and installed, we put her handprints on the door, symbolically holding it open. If you ever see the Witness Blanket in person and find yourself walking through the doorway, look down at the lower part of the door. You will see two little handprints in black paint, right at kid height, pushing the door from the inside. They are Adelyn's. She made them when she was about four years old, the same age as many kids who were forced to go to residential school.

CAREY NEWMAN

Eventually I put it in a door frame and placed it at the center of the Blanket. Partly because of the abuse that took place in the St. Michael's boys' infirmary, but also because of the different kinds of tragic and terrible things that happened in residential schools, often behind closed doors, I decided that I didn't ever want the door on the Blanket to be closed. Every once in a while I would walk into the studio and find the door closed. I would always open it. Eventually I made a doorstop. Now, whenever the Witness Blanket is on display, I make sure the door is always open so there is nowhere for any secrets to hide.

BRICK

Contributor **ANGELINE AYOUNGMAN**
Location **OLD SUN RESIDENTIAL SCHOOL, GLEICHEN, AB**

opposite: JESSICA SIGURDSON, CANADIAN MUSEUM FOR HUMAN RIGHTS

Fitting the Pieces Together ♦ 71

10 RECONCILIATION IS A JOURNEY

BACK AT THE VERY beginning, when I was sitting in my living room with my feet on that small folding stool, the Witness Blanket was just an idea or a dream. If I were to speak my truth, I'd say that deep inside me, I thought by making this Blanket I would be stitching together pieces of reconciliation itself.

What I realize now is that back then I didn't yet understand the meaning of reconciliation. The more I learned about the truth of what happened at residential schools, the intergenerational trauma that followed and the historical and ongoing effects of colonialism, the better I understood the size and complexity of the issues that reconciliation must address.

opposite: ALYSSA O'CONNOR

Carey speaks at the CMHR after signing an agreement to place the Blanket under its stewardship. COURTESY OF THE CANADIAN MUSEUM FOR HUMAN RIGHTS

> "I will always remember, because through all of this I have been changed. And I think that is the truth about reconciliation. We don't change each other. The responsibility is individual. It happens inside each of us, by our own actions and decisions, one human at a time."
>
> CAREY NEWMAN

Everyone in Canada Is Equal

I now understand that truth must come before reconciliation, and that reconciliation is not limited to social repairs like providing clean water and equal access to healthcare and education. Those are basic human rights. Lasting reconciliation needs to be about disrupting the colonial systems that created these problems in the first place. It is about respect for this land, respect for each other and recognizing all humans who live in Canada as equal.

At first that realization left me feeling overwhelmed, as though the problems were too big and too many to overcome. But then I started to think about how much I had learned about myself. That was when I began to understand that reconciliation is a journey rather than an act or a destination. Although I don't necessarily feel less conflicted about the experience of growing up part Indigenous and part settler, my knowing the

factors that led to that turmoil in the first place is a step toward reconciling all the parts of who I am.

Listening to the Stories

I'm not sure if it comes from the pain and power that are held with truth, the fragments of hope that slowly build, one upon another, or the whispers of my **ancestors**, but I have begun to realize that we each bear

above: The Heart Garden was planted at Rideau Hall in Ottawa, ON, for the closing ceremonies of the Truth and Reconciliation Commission on June 3, 2015. MEDIA ONE INC. *below:* In many residential schools boys worked outside, gardening and maintaining the grounds. GENERAL SYNOD ARCHIVES, ANGLICAN CHURCH OF CANADA

The legal agreement between Survivors, churches and the Government of Canada led to the creation of the Truth and Reconciliation Commission. As the TRC administered money that Survivors had designated for commemoration projects like the Witness Blanket, the Blanket was actually funded by residential school Survivors themselves.

Reconciliation Is a Journey ♦ 75

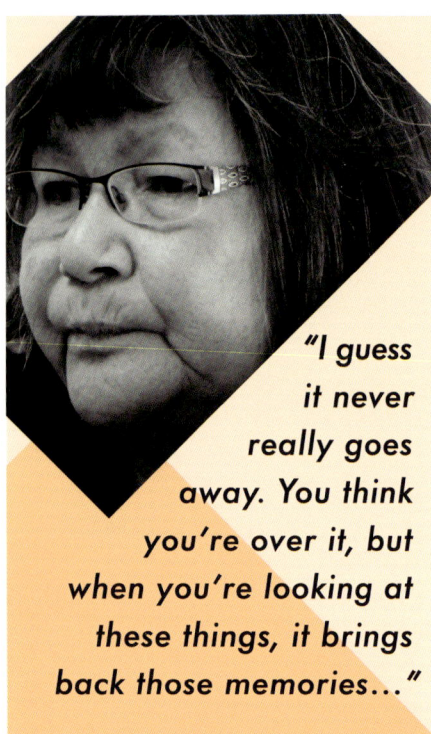

"I guess it never really goes away. You think you're over it, but when you're looking at these things, it brings back those memories…"

Survivor **ANGELINE AYOUNGMAN** on seeing the dormitory at the Old Sun Community College in Alberta, the site of her former residential school

"When I've finished a piece of art, I ask a spiritual person to cleanse it to prepare it for the next part of its journey. They do this with a ceremony where traditional medicine like dried sage, braided sweetgrass or crushed cedar or tobacco is slowly burned. The smoke is called the smudge, and it cleanses the spirit of anything it touches."

CAREY NEWMAN

PIANO KEYS
Contributor **LEON WOLFE**
Location **MUSCOWEQUAN RESIDENTIAL SCHOOL, LESTOCK, SK**

witness by our own experiences. We are responsible for learning from and remembering them.

The pieces on the Witness Blanket each represent a different story, a different person and a different place. Through the stories of a few Survivors we begin to understand the stories of all Survivors. The idea was that these everyday objects would communicate in a different language, connecting each of us through our own memories and experience. That their presence would recall residential schools themselves, somehow making them more tangible. That the enduring spirit within these bits and parts would form something undeniable, a heartbeat that would gently and resolutely command our attention.

In the traditions of my Coast Salish ancestors, a blanket is gifted to uplift the spirit, protect the vulnerable or honor the strong.

♦ I made this Blanket for the Survivors and for the children who never came home, for the displaced and the forgotten.

♦ It is for the parents who hold their stories inside, afraid of how the truth might affect their children.

♦ It is for those who are angry, those who are in pain and those who are bitter.

♦ It is for those who remember and those who are still trying to forget.

♦ To forget the braids that were shorn, the dignity that was stolen and the beatings, abuse and violation.

♦ I made this Blanket so that I will never forget—so that we will never forget.

♦ It is for families who have lost their aunts and uncles and sisters and brothers and mothers and fathers and children.

♦ It is for those who left us too soon. We have all lost someone too soon.

♦ I made this for the communities that were broken, their future scooped up and sent away, silence replacing the sound of children's laughter.

Students with their teacher on the steps of the Round Lake residential school in Saskatchewan in the 1940s. UCCA (93.049P1162/ROUND LAKE IRS CIRCA 1940)

Carey's grandparents with (left to right) Carey's uncle Chuck, aunt Myrtle and aunt Georgina. COURTESY OF THE NEWMAN FAMILY

Students and staff in front of St. Paul's residential school on the Blood Reserve, 1924. GLENBOW ARCHIVES (ND-27-48)

Susan and Elizabeth Mitchell on the Union Steamship Company boat, going back to residential school. COURTESY OF MICHELLE WASHINGTON

♦ It is for the victims of violence and the perpetrators of that same violence, some of whom were never taught a better way.

♦ It is for those like me, who didn't know how much we were affected until we tried to speak our traditional languages or sing our traditional songs, who didn't know what we didn't know.

♦ It is for those who found, when they had children of their own, that they had to learn how to show them love. I love my daughter, my only child, but I was afraid to have a son for fear that I wouldn't know how to relate to him. That is the way it was for many years between my father and me.

♦ It is for those of us who spent parts of our lives ashamed of our heritage. For those who have yet to learn to respect themselves for who they are and where they are from.

♦ I made this for our cultures, our languages and our traditions.

♦ It is for the governments and churches who tried to take them from us.

♦ It is for everyone who held on to those traditions, passing them on through generations so they are able to flourish again.

♦ I made this for anyone who doesn't know what a residential school is or the truth of what happened there.

♦ I made this Blanket for the people who want to learn. For those who walk beside us and those who are only now ready to walk beside us.

♦ I made this for the conversations to come, for the lessons we have yet to learn and for the future we are building together.

♦ I made this Blanket for hope. I made it for truth. I made it to catch our tears. I made it for me and I made it for each of you.

♦ It is for our children, our children's children and every generation to come.

♦ It is for my daughter.

♦ But from the very beginning this Blanket was inspired by, and has always been for, my father.

above: Carey's daughter, Adelyn, in front of the finished Witness Blanket. JESSE HLADY

left: Carey and his father, Victor, after the Blanket was finished. BRUCE MARTIN

WOVEN IN

Making the Witness Blanket tested me in many ways. The personal, artistic and emotional challenges were far greater than I ever anticipated. I often think that if, at the very start, I had known about everything I would have to accomplish in order to complete the project, I would never have believed it was possible. But with perseverance and the help of many people, I saw it through. While many things didn't turn out exactly as I had planned, the changes were mostly for the better, and what started out as an idea about making a blanket from bricks and stone and metal turned into much more.

JESSE HLADY

I am no longer the same man as the one who began this project. I watched the weight lift from my father's shoulders as he returned to the site of the last residential school he attended. I saw my family draw closer as we shared his journey. I watched my daughter grow, and I considered her place in all of this. I heard stories that broke me into pieces and stories that put me back together. I laughed, I cried, and every so often I cry some more. I have been enriched by the beauty and generosity of people I met along the way, those who made the Witness Blanket a reality, who created meaning through their stories and spirit, their work and patience. I am humbled by their trust.

Reconciliation Is a Journey

GLOSSARY

ancestors—family members who lived before your oldest living relative was born

CBC—Canadian Broadcasting Corporation, Canada's publicly owned radio and television broadcaster

collective truth—the idea that when many individual stories are put together, they add up to undeniable truth

colonization—the imposition by people from one culture of their own political, legal and social systems on people from another culture, in an attempt to steal land from them and extinguish their rights

Cree syllabics—the system of letters and symbols used to write in the Cree language

day schools—schools created with the same intention as residential schools, the difference being that students were permitted to go home every day

JESSE HLADY

Department of Indian Affairs—the branch of the federal government that attempted to control all aspects of Indigenous life in Canada (today two departments, Crown-Indigenous Relations and Northern Affairs Canada, and Indigenous Services Canada)

Elder—a title used in some Indigenous cultures that reflects both the age and wisdom of a person

Indian Residential School Settlement Agreement (IRSSA)—the legal agreement between the Government of Canada and residential school Survivors that provided the framework for all aspects of the largest class-action settlement in Canadian history

Indigenous Peoples—in Canada this term is most commonly used to collectively describe First Nations, Métis and Inuit

industrial schools—residential schools that used students as unpaid child labor

infirmary—a room where sick or injured students were treated

Intergenerational Survivors—descendants of residential school Survivors who are in some way affected by the experience of those Survivors

intergenerational trauma—the impacts of trauma passed down from residential school Survivors to their descendants

National Centre for Truth and Reconciliation—an archive of testimony, objects and documentation that relates to the residential school era in Canada

portage—the work of carrying a canoe and any goods over land from one waterway to another or around some obstacle

Potlatch—a traditional gathering practiced in some Indigenous communities, in which people come together to deal with social, political, spiritual and cultural issues through ceremony

reconciliation—in this book, reconciliation refers to the process of acknowledging and repairing the harms inflicted on Indigenous people by colonization

regalia—traditional attire that is worn in ceremonies, varying from one Indigenous culture to another

reserve—land designated by the federal government, through the Indian Act, for the exclusive use of First Nations people

residential school—a school system, imposed by the Canadian government and run by churches, that removed Indigenous children from their communities with the intention of extinguishing family and cultural connections

settlers—people who live in Canada but whose ancestors originally came from another country

Sixties Scoop—a legacy of the residential school system in which a disproportionate number of Indigenous children were taken from their families and communities and adopted or placed in foster care

Survivor—an Indigenous person who endured the residential school system and all the effects and trauma of that experience

totem pole—a Northwest Coast Indigenous art form, typically carved from cedar, that depicts stories, families or significant events

Truth and Reconciliation Commission of Canada (TRC)—a commission established through the IRSSA as a means to record and document the experiences of residential school Survivors and begin the process of Canada's reconciliation with Indigenous Peoples

opposite: JESSICA SIGURDSON, CANADIAN MUSEUM FOR HUMAN RIGHTS

RESOURCES

Akiwenzie-Damm and Sonny Assu, Brandon Mitchell, Rachel Qitsualik-Tinsley, Sean Qitsualik-Tinsley, David A. Robertson, Niigaanwewidam James Sinclair, Jen Storm, Richard Van Camp, Katherena Vermette, Chelsea Vowel. *This Place: 150 Years Retold.* Highwater Press, 2019.

Campbell, Nicola I. *Shin-chi's Canoe.* Groundwood Books/House of Anansi Press, 2008.

Dimaline, Cherie. *The Marrow Thieves.* Cormorant Books, 2017.

Dupuis, Jenny Kay, and Kathy Kacer. *I Am Not a Number.* Second Story Press, 2016.

Florence, Melanie. *Stolen Words.* Second Story Press, 2017.

Gray Smith, Monique. *Speaking Our Truth: A Journey of Reconciliation.* Orca Book Publishers, 2017.

Jordan-Fenton, Christy, and Margaret Pokiak-Fenton. *Fatty Legs: A True Story.* Annick Press, 2010.

Jordan-Fenton, Christy, and Margaret Pokiak-Fenton. *Not My Girl.* Annick Press, 2014.

Jordan-Fenton, Christy, and Margaret Pokiak-Fenton. *Stranger at Home: A True Story.* Annick Press, 2011.

JESSE HLADY

Kinew, Wab. *Go Show the World*. Tundra Books, 2018.

Loyie, Larry, and Constance Brissenden. *As Long As the River Flows*. Groundwood Books/House of Anansi Press, 2005.

Robertson, David Alexander. *The Barren Grounds: The Misewa Saga, Book One*. Puffin Canada, 2021.

Robertson, David Alexander. *Sugar Falls: A Residential School Story*. Portage and Main Press, 2012.

Sellars, Bev. *They Called Me Number One: Secrets and Survival at an Indian Residential School*. Talonbooks, 2012.

Smith, Cynthia Leitich ed. *Ancestor Approved: Intertribal Stories for Kids*. Heartdrum, 2021.

External resources are for personal and/or educational use only and are provided in good faith without any express or implied warranty. There is no guarantee given as to the accuracy or currency of any individual item. The authors and publisher provide the resources as a service to readers. This does not imply any endorsement by the authors or publisher of any of the content contained in these works.

JESSICA SIGURDSON,
CANADIAN MUSEUM FOR HUMAN RIGHTS

ACKNOWLEDGMENTS

We would like to begin by acknowledging that most of this book was written on the traditional unceded territories of the Lekwungen People.

Although it is impossible to acknowledge the confluence of efforts and circumstances that have made this book possible, we would like to single out some individuals for their contributions.

We raise our hands:

- To Victor Newman and all the other residential school Survivors who not only shared the personal stories that fill these pages but also contributed the physical pieces that became the Witness Blanket. *Gilakas'la* for your generosity and courage.

- To each of the Intergenerational Survivors who shared their reflections and experiences that continue to increase awareness and understanding of the ongoing impacts of colonialism.

- To the collection, construction and cultural teams, our friends and colleagues, and all of the organizations, institutions and funders that have contributed to making the Witness Blanket and empowering the many related projects and initiatives that continue to develop.

- To everyone at Orca Book Publishers who helped turn this book and its older sibling into a reality.

- And to our families, for giving us the time, space and support to get this story just right.

INDEX

Page numbers in **bold** indicate an image caption.

Aklavik residential school (NT), 61
Alberni residential school (Port Alberni, BC), 45
Aller, Robert, 45, 47
Allison, Marilyn (Murray), 28–30
All Saints residential school (Lac La Ronge, SK), 35
Alphonse, Shirley, 58, 60
Arctic schools, **39**
art classes, 41, 45, **47**
assimilation, 3, 11, 60–62
Ayoungman, Angeline, 16, 31, 76

Bishop Horden Hall residential school (Moose Factory, ON), 51–53
Blanchet, Cyrus, **11**
blankets, significance, 5–6, 76
Blood Reserve residential school (AB), **38**, **46**, **63**, **78**
bowls and dishes, 19, 21
bricks, 11, 18, 19, **71**
Bryce, Peter, 23
buildings
    floor plans, 18
    after school closures, 50, 66, 68

Canada
    moving forward, 62, 74–76
    nutrition studies by, 22, 23
    policies, 2–3, 11
    regulation of schools, 51–53
    role of government, 3, 11, 62, 75
    Sixties Scoop, 59, 84

Canadian Museum for Human Rights (Winnipeg, MA), 62, **74**
canoe carving, 53
canoeing accident, 51–53
Carpenter, John, 52, 53
Catholic Church, 2
ceremonies
    hair-cutting, 58–60, 61
    regalia, 36, 84
    smudging, 76
Charlie, Bob, 45–47
Chief Moon, Keith, 10
children
    isolation of, 14–15, 35, 37
    loss of cultural identity, 53–54
    and native language, 3, 78
    relationship with family, 4, 60–63
    separation from family, 39
    sharing stolen food, 23
    Sixties Scoop, 59, 84
Chooutla residential school (Carcross, YT), 14–16, **18**
Christie residential school (Kakawis, BC), 23–24
churches, role of, 3, 11, 62, 75
clothing
    a child's shoe, 13, 15–16, **18**, 19
    and identity, 61
    moccasins, 19, 27, 31
    in photographs, 33, 34
    school uniforms, 29
    taken away, 28
collective truth, 17, 75–76, 82
colonization, 2–3, 62, 74, 82
Coon, Mary, 28
Coppermine Tent Hostel (Kugluktuk, NU), **39**

Coqualeetza residential school (Chilliwack, BC), 33–38
Cree syllabics, 51, 82
Crow Chief, Charlie, 63
cultural heritage. *see also* ceremonies
    and blankets, 5–6, 76
    and government policy, 3, 11
    and identity, 53–54, 61
    loss of language, 3, 78
    Potlatches, 7, 84
    wood carving, 4–5, 53

day schools, 38, 82
deaths
    canoeing accident, 51–53
    grave sites, 7, 31, 52
    illness, 29–31
Department of Indian Affairs, 22, 23, 51–53, 83
documents, 49–55
Dodman, Florence Mary, 28–30
dolls, **45**
door, infirmary, 65–71
doorknob, 19, **35**
dormitories, 47, **63**

Edmonds, Ambrose, **50**
Edmonton industrial school (St. Albert, AB), 27, 43
education, attendance laws, 39
Elders, 60, 62, 83
Elkhorn residential school (MB), 53

families
    loss of cultural identity, 53–54
    loss of relationships, 60–63
    and parenting skills, 62–63

families (continued)
   and separation, 4, 35, 39
   siblings, 29–31
farming, industrial schools, 25, 27
food
   memory of, 21–24, 29
   for staff, priests and nuns, 23–24, 25, 29
Fort Albany, (ON), 55

gardening, **75**
Gatensby, Harold, 14–15
glass pieces, 10
Gordon's residential school (Punnichy, SK), 42, 46, **59**
graduation certificates, 50
grave sites, 7, 31, 52

hair-cutting ceremony, 58–60, 61
Hartman, Rosy, **11**, 13, **14**, 15–16, **18**
health conditions
   illness, 29–31
   inadequate nutrition, 21–24
hockey, 42–43, 47
hockey skates, 19, 43, 44

identity
   and culture, 53–54, 61
   and self-esteem, 14, 37
illness, 29–31
Immaculate Conception residential school (Aklavik, NT), 61
Indian Residential School Settlement Agreement (IRSSA), 62, 83
Indigenous Peoples, 2, 83
industrial schools
   defined, 83
   skills training, 25, 27, 29
infirmary, 65, 68, 83
Intergenerational Survivors
   defined, 4, 61, 83
   living with respect, 74–76
   telling their story, 11, 73

Jordan-Fenton, Christy, 60

Kamloops residential school (BC), grave sites, 52
Keptana, Lucy, 50

Lac La Ronge residential school (SK), 35, 37, 39
lamp, brass, **52**
language
   Cree syllabics, 51, 82
   divide between parents and child, 60–62
   loss of, 3, 78
Lejac residential school (Fraser Lake, BC), 42
Lesser Slave Lake residential school (AB), 34
letters, 51–55
Lewis, Jamie, **11**
Little Buffalo residential school (Lubicon Lake, AB), **22**
Lucas, Richard, 23

Macdonald, John A., 11
MacKenzie, A.J., **51**, 52
merit badges, 19, 30
Metatawabin, Edmund, 68
Mission residential school (BC), **50**
Mitchell, Susan and Elizabeth, **78**
moccasins, 19, 27, 29, 31
Mohawk Institute residential school (Brantford, ON), 21, 25, 67
Mosby, Ian, 22
Muscowequan residential school (Lestock, SK), 45
music, 41, **46**

National Centre for Truth and Reconciliation, 51, 84
Nelson, Anne, 27
Newman, Adelyn, 71, **79**
Newman, Carey
   about, 1, 2, 3, 4–5, 22–23

Newman, Carey (continued)
   on impact of objects, 13, 16, 17
   and the infirmary door, 65–71
   personal journey of, 77–81
   on reconciliation, 74–76
Newman, Elaine, 6–7, 24
Newman, Ellen, 57, 58–60, 61
Newman, Marion, 57, 58–60
Newman, Victor
   about, 2, 3, 68, **79**
   experience of, 22, 61
   the photographs of, 36, 57
Newman family
   objects from, 36, 57–60, **62**
   photos of, **3**, 77
Nunavut, 10
nutrition, inadequate, 21–24

objects
   as collective truth, 17, 18–19, 75–76
   reactions to, 15–16, 17
   as silent witness, 6–7, 19, 25, 31
Ottawa, (ON), Heart Garden, **75**

Parnell, Jerome, 57
photographs
   image blocks, **37**
   as silent witness, 33–38, 44
   and sports, 42–44
piano keys, 19, **76**
Pokiak-Fenton, Margaret, 60
Potlatches, 7, 84

racism. *see* colonization
reconciliation
   defined, 84
   journey, 60, 61, 73–75
regalia, 36, 84
relationships
   language barriers, 3, 60, 78
   parent-child, 4, 35, 39, 60–63
reserves, 53, 84
residential schools
   boat travel to, 35, **78**

residential schools (continued)
   classrooms, **38**
   dining rooms, **22**, 24
   dormitories, 47, **63**
   first day, 28, 37, 61
   floor plans, 18
   infirmary, 65, 68, 83
   lack of good food, 22–23, 54
   skills training, 25, 27, 29, **75**
   sports and play, 41–47
   strict rules of, 22, 24, 29–30
   unmarked graves, 7, 31, 52
   use of sites, 66, 68
residential school system
   about, 3–4, 38, 84
   attendance laws, 39
resources, 86
Roberts, Tom, 35, 37–38, 39, 69
Round Lake residential school (SK), 77

school records, 50
schools. *see* residential schools
school uniform sweater, 29
Sechelt residential school (BC), 25, 61, 68
settlers, 1, 2, 11, 84
shoes, a child's, **12**, 13, 15–16, **17**, **18**, 19
sign, metal, **59**
Sinclair, Murray, 23
Sixties Scoop, 59, 84
skills training, 27, 29
   merit badges, 19, 30
sports and play
   broomball, 44
   dolls, 45
   hockey, 42–43, 47
St. Eugene Mission (Cranbrook, BC), 10
St. Joseph's residential school (Fort Resolution, NT), 28–30, **31**
St. Jude's Cathedral, (Iqaluit, NU), 10, **11**
St. Mary's residential school (Blood Reserve, AB), **38**

St. Mary's residential school (Mission, BC), **2**, **9**, 68
St. Michael's residential school (Alert Bay, BC), **6**, **52**, 53–54, 65–71
storytelling
   and collective truth, 17, 75–76, 82
   and objects, 10, 11, 18–19
St. Paul's residential school (Blood Reserve, AB), **78**
St. Peter's Anglican Mission (Lesser Slave Lake, AB), 34
Stranger at Home, 60
Survivors. *see also* trauma
   bearing witness, 6–7, 75–76
   children of, 11, 60–63, 74–76
   commemoration projects, 75
   defined, 84
   memory of food, 21–24
   memory of sports, 41
   speaking up, 47
   telling their story, 10, 11, 38–39
sweaters, 29
sweetgrass, braided, **16**, 76

teachers and staff
   food for staff, priests and nuns, 23–24, 25
   lack of accountability, 51–53
   in photographs, 34
tents, 39
Thompson, Art, 45, 47
totem poles, 5, 84
toys, 45
trauma
   and bad memories, 13, 68
   death of sister, 29–31
   and eating habits, 22–24
   leaving home, 35, 68
   and relationships, 3–4, 60–63
trophies, 42
Truth and Reconciliation Commission of Canada (TRC), 4, 6, 75, 84

Victoria Native Friendship Centre (Victoria, BC), 10

Wamiss, Nancy, 24, 53–54
Wamiss, Stan, 53–54
Whitefish Lake residential school (AB), 34
Whitehorse Baptist Mission residential school (YT), 45
Witness Blanket coins, 7
Witness Blanket collection team, **5**, 7–10, 19, 49
Witness Blanket project
   concept, 5–6, 9, 49
   dedication, 77–79
   design, 25, 29, 36, 65–66
   door symbolism, 71
   funding, 75
   making, 8, 16, 17, 18–19, 80–81
   as permanent record, 50–51
   and reconciliation, 73–75
   size of, 9
Wolfe, Leon, 43
Woomastoogish, (Chief), 51–53

yearbooks, 50
Yukon schools, 14, 15, 45

CAREY NEWMAN or Hayalthkin'geme is a multi-disciplinary artist and master carver. Through his father he is Kwakw<u>a</u>ka'wakw from the Kukwekum, Giiksam and WaWalaby'ie clans of Fort Rupert, and Coast Salish from Cheam of the Stó:lo Nation along the upper Fraser Valley. Through his mother he is English, Irish and Scottish. In his artistic practice he strives to highlight Indigenous, social or environmental issues. Carey was awarded the Meritorious Service Medal in 2017 and was named to the Order of British Columbia in 2018. Carey lives in Victoria, British Columbia.

KIRSTIE HUDSON is an editor and writer in Victoria, British Columbia. She was a reporter and producer with the CBC in Toronto, Vancouver, Prince Rupert and Victoria. In her award-winning career as a journalist, Kirstie's work was recognized with a Jack Webster Award, Radio Television Digital News Association Awards and a Gabriel Award. As an instructor at the University of Victoria and Royal Roads University, Kirstie shared her love of storytelling with students in writing, communications and journalism.

Together, Carey and Kirstie wrote *Picking Up the Pieces: Residential School Memories and the Making of the Witness Blanket*, which was a finalist for the City of Victoria Butler Book Prize and the Norma Fleck Award for Canadian Children's Nonfiction.

The Witness Blanket now lives at the Canadian Museum for Human Rights (CMHR) in Winnipeg, Manitoba. It was placed there through a unique stewardship agreement between Carey and the CMHR. The agreement recognizes the legal rights of the Blanket and the stories it holds and shares responsibility for its care between Carey and the CMHR. For more information, please visit humanrights.ca.